Published by the
American Sailing Association
and International Marine
10 9 8 7 6 5 4 3 2 1

Questions regarding the contents of
this book should be addressed to:
American Sailing Association
13922 Marquesas Way
Marina del Rey, CA 90292
(310) 822–7171 Phone
(310) 822–4741 Fax
ouch9@cinenet.net Email
http://www.american–sailing.com World Wide Web

Questions regarding the ordering of this book
should be addressed to:
The McGraw–Hill Companies
Customer Service Department
P.O. Box 547
Blacklick, OH 43004
Retail customers: 1-800-262-4729
Bookstores: 1-800-722-4726

MULTIHULL CRUISING

FUNDAMENTALS

by

Rick White

Editor/Project Manager

Harry Munns

Illustrations/Design

Kevin Allen Pike

International Marine Camden, Maine

Photos

Jim Heffelfinger
Ray Bassett

Technical Review

Jim Heffelfinger
Pat Reischmann

Text Editor

Cindy Wise

*The American Sailing Association
acknowledges the following
(in no special order) for their invaluable
help with the creation of this book.*

Manta Enterprises of Largo, FL
Pat Reischmann
Richard and Penny Flaherty
Christopher Rodgerson
Pacific Sailing of Marina del Rey, CA
Mike Lenneman
Multi Marine of Marina del Rey, CA
Shirley Warner
Molly Mulhern
Jonathan Eaton
International Marine Publishing
PARA–TECH Engineering Co.

The American Sailing Association works through sailors, sailing instructors, sailing schools and charter fleets throughout North America. Our purpose is to bring organization and professional standards to sailing education. Boating safety through education has been our goal since we were founded over a decade ago.

The ASA International Log Book contains the comprehensive sailing standards which represent the heart of the ASA system. These performance objectives give sailors a set of goals and a means by which to gauge their knowledge and abilities. Certified professional sailing instructors administer the standards at ASA sailing schools. Through certification to these standards the ASA provides the individual with a reliable way to document achievement in sailing.

The ASA International Log Book contains a detailed list of requirements for each standard, space to affix certification seals and a record of sailing experience. Sailors use the Log Book as their personal passport and sailing autobiography. Charter companies and rental operations worldwide recognize the quality of the ASA standards and accept the ASA Log Book as proof of knowledge and experience.

ASA sailing schools get thousands of new sailors started each year. Increasing numbers of experienced sailors have begun to "challenge" the ASA standards. They are tested on their knowledge and ability without the necessity of attending classes. ASA certifications are then awarded for the appropriate certification levels.

The ASA has made a positive difference in the quality of American sailing education. With the continued support of professional sailing schools and instructors our work will expand and grow.

We commend the growing number of people who improve their knowledge and enjoyment of sailing through the ASA system and its various elements, including *Multihull Cruising Fundamentals*.

TABLE OF CONTENTS

CHAPTERS 1 THROUGH 4
TRAILERABLE MULTIHULLS

CHAPTERS 5 THROUGH 8
CRUISING CATAMARANS

Nautical historians trace origins of the multihull back as far as two thousand years before Columbus sailed to the new world. While some evidence exists of ancient multihull construction in what is now the Middle East and Asia, Polynesian peoples made the most visible mark in the chronicles of multihull antiquity.

Early examples of vessels with more than one hull were little more than a couple of hollowed–out logs held together with smaller tree branches. Historians theorize that ancient Polynesians used these early multihulls to populate islands and continents thousands of miles distant from their home-lands.

The 1950s, 60s and 70s saw a revival of interest in design and construction of recreational vessels with multiple hulls. Most of the visionaries who sought to bridge the historical gap between modern pleasure boat-ing and ancient Polynesian seafaring built experimental vessels, often with dubious results. Many of these early experiments were created without the engineering expertise of naval architects. Due to some relatively iso-lated structural failures, multihulls of this era gained a reputation as being unsafe.

The speed, stability and comfort of multihulls helped this ancient concept tran-scend the damaging blow that this 20th cen-tury evolutionary incarnation had dealt it. In the 80s and 90s reputable manufacturers took notice of multihulls and created a new gener-ation of sound, attractive and seaworthy cruising multihulls.

Today's sailing consumers can choose from an ever–expanding fleet of high–quality, commercially produced multihulls. They have gone from novelty items for counter–culture radicals to a viable, attractive option for boat buyers and charterers throughout the world.

Multihull Cruising Fundamentals unlocks the secrets of these often misunder-stood vessels. It was written for curious sailors who seek thrills not only in their sail-ing experiences, but in the boats they sail. Who else would be drawn to a style of boat that started out as a couple of hollowed–out logs, then, thousands of years later, became a backyard science project, only to transform into a phenomenon that still makes tradi-tionalists scratch their heads in bewilder-ment?

The Book is divided into two sec-tions: Trailerable Multihulls and Cruising Catamarans. Trailerable catamarans and tri-marans within the 20 to 30 foot range have become tremendously popular in recent years. Section I provides readers with the skills and knowledge necessary to safely operate these new and exciting pleasure boats.

Section II examines the other phe-nomenon in modern multihull technology, cruising catamarans. These fast, comfortable vessels range between 30 and 50 feet. Section II teaches readers what they need to know to enter the world in which these big cats rule.

Section I provides the background for achieving ASA Trailerable Multihull (113) certification while Section II prepares readers for the Cruising Catamaran (114) standard.

SECTION I
TRAILERABLE MULTIHULLS

CHAPTER I

GETTING ACQUAINTED

SAILING KNOWLEDGE

"In the Marquesas, for instance, the tree from which the hull was to be made was felled to the tune of the creation chant, an extremely sacred element of the liturgy. The tree was hewn where it fell, a sacred building being constructed over it to protect it and shelter the workmen."

The Island Civilizations of Polynesia
– Robert C. Suggs

Every new boat presents unique and exciting qualities and challenges. Sailors who choose to explore unfamiliar boats expand their knowledge and experience in ways they may not even realize. When the entire design and construction of a new boat differs dramatically from the familiar, lessons become richer and more rewarding.

The best way to get started is to take a look around and see what we do and do not recognize.

TOPSIDE ORIENTATION

Catamarans have two hulls and trimarans have three. Both catamarans and trimarans are referred to under the larger heading of multihulls. It follows then that boats with only one hull are monohulls.

The trimaran's middle hull is referred to as the main hull. The outer hulls are called amas.

The term "ama" dates back to the ancient Polynesians and is still widely used. So, you have an ama on each side of the main hull. There are a few designers that refer to the amas as floats, but that expression is not very well acknowledged in the multihull sailing world.

Catamarans just have a port and starboard hull although, while under sail, you are much more likely to hear the hulls referred to as windward or leeward.

CLIMBING ABOARD

With our boat tied abeam to the dock, your first step aboard a catamaran will be onto one of the hulls. On a trimaran, you will step onto one of the amas. By the way, neither boat design will tip much under your weight. The catamaran will hardly move at all. Some of the smaller trimarans with less buoyancy in their amas might sink a little with the first step. As we will see later, wide beams help make multihulls of the 20 to 30 foot size range extremely stable compared to monohulls. However, it would be

The catamaran's two hulls support the bridge deck between them. The dolphin striker (inset) extends between the main hull and ama of this trimaran.

Catamaran rigs exert tremendous downward pressure on the main beam through the mast. The wind's force is transferred from the rig to the boat, creating motion. Most of that force reaches the boat at the base of the mast. As breezes freshen and sails are sheeted harder, the mast packs more of a downward punch.

All sailboat masts exert a lot of downward pressure. Monohull masts exert force on the keel, a very substantial struc-

ture. But, since there is only a long, unsupported bridge area between a catamaran's hulls, an extension of the mast is often needed to go below the main beam. Stainless steel strapping or cables run from the area where the main beam

prudent to grab a shroud to steady yourself as you step onto any boat.

TOPSIDE CONSTRUCTION

All multihulls bind their hulls together with structurally sound cross members. On catamarans they are called cross beams. The main beam is located forward and usually supports the mast. The aft or rear beam supports the stern of the boat and normally has the main sheet and traveler attached to it.

The cross members on a trimaran are often referred to as cross beams as well, but more often they are referred to as akas, another Polynesian word. Again, there is a main aka and an aft aka.

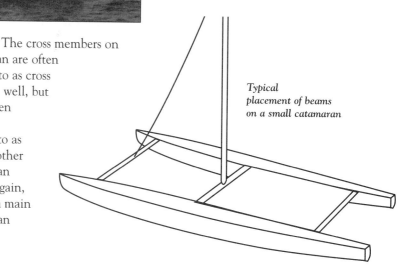

Typical placement of beams on a small catamaran

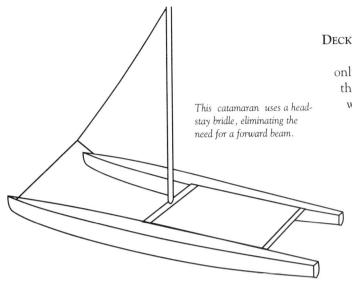

This catamaran uses a head-stay bridle, eliminating the need for a forward beam.

DECKS

Catamarans have only one deck, called the bridge deck, which spans the gap between the hulls. It can be an open deck made of netting or trampoline material, or it can be a closed deck made of a material such as fiberglass or wood.

On trimarans the span between the main hull and each ama is referred to as a

deck (all solid material).

An open wing deck with netting or tramp material is much lighter, and most multihull sailors strive to keep weight off the boat. The drawback is that it can be a little difficult to walk on – sort of like trying to walk on a bouncing trampoline. Open wing decks also let water flow through. Getting splashed can be a treat on a hot day, but most other times people prefer to stay dry. Water will not collect, however, so if you do get

Wing deck (above) made of trampoline material. Base of a pivoting mast (left).

splashed you have a good chance of drying out.

The full wing deck allows for better footing and easier walking; however, it is heavy. Heavy is not good on multihulls. Water will not come up from below, but certain parts of the deck may collect small pools depending on the angle of heel.

A full wing deck can also generate lift when air passes above and below it. Partial wing decks don't have this problem. The partial wing deck obviously combines some of the positives and negatives of both types of decking. It will be up to individual sailors to decide what fits their performance and comfort expectations.

attaches to each hull and support the mast extension's downward thrust. This apparatus looks like a traditional bow sprit support turned sideways. It is called a dolphin striker, probably because it hits the water sometimes in seas. Watch out Flipper!

Some catamarans have a third beam. This beam is near the bow and is called the forward beam. The forestay attaches to the beam, causing a lot of upward force on this span. Depending on the design, it may take a very hefty forward beam to resist the upward thrust. (Refer to Seagull Striker in Section II, Cruising Catamarans.)

So, to keep weight off the bow, many cats use a headstay bridle. Instead of a beam, they simply attach a short length of stainless steel rigging cable to each bow. The forestay attaches to both cables at a spot (carefully calculated by engineers) somewhere above deck level forming a bridle. Although some of the force in this set–up pulls the hulls together, there is neither direct upward force nor direct lateral force and the structure of the boat can easily withstand the forces.

wing deck. This can be an open wing deck (all netting or trampoline material), a partial wing deck (partial solid material and partial netting/trampoline), or full wing

Trimarans often use a netting material between the main hull bow and the ama bows ahead of the main crossbeam or aka. These are referred to as safety nets. You should move very carefully on the nets. They are used primarily for emergencies. What kind of emergency you might ask? Almost falling off the bow would be a good example.

RIGGING

Standing rigging on a trailerable multi performs about the same tasks and looks similar to that of a monohull. Mast, boom, shrouds and stays will look familiar. On closer inspection, however, you may notice some differences.

Some production multihulls have rotating masts. These spars pivot at the base when the mainsail fills and the sail is pushed to leeward. Their flat surfaces then align with the sail's luff. Air then flows much more smoothly across the mainsail's surface and performance improves.

Sailors will also discover that shrouds, which they rarely touch on monohulls, need attention on some multihulls. Folding trimarans, for example, will have their upper shrouds attached to the amas. Folding and unfolding amas requires some care to keep shrouds out of the way. You may also find cap shroud tensioners which allow you to tension the upper shrouds using block and tackle from the cockpit area.

Another innovative and fairly exotic feature found on today's smaller multis is the roller furling boom. Just as the name suggests, the boom rotates 360°, rolling and unrolling the mainsail like a window shade. In most cases, the winch handle fits into the aft end of the boom for

Typical tiller/rudder on a trimaran. Designers make best use of available interior space.

furling. It unfurls as the halyard raises the mainsail to the top of the mast.

NOTE: The boom angle must be nearly perpendicular to the mast or sail raising could become difficult.

STEERING

Production monohulls in the 25 to 30 foot range can come with either wheel or tiller steering. Wheel steering seems to be the method preferred by most prospective buyers.

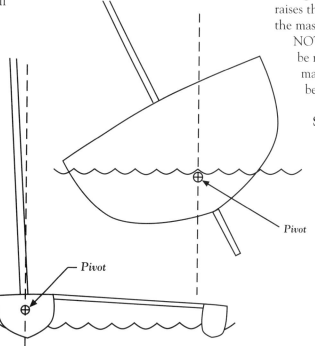

Ama flotation, counterbalance from the windward ama and sheer breadth all keep the trimaran sailing flat.

Pivot

Pivot

1 The relationship between car and trailer is similar to the relationship between tiller and boat. For example, when the car backs to the left the trailer turns to the right.

2 Turning the steering wheel in one direction will cause the trailer to turn in the opposite direction.

3 It is best to set your car and trailer up as straight as possible relative to the launch ramp prior to backing toward the ramp.

4 Back slowly and spot changes in backing angles as soon as they begin.

5 Corrections in angles should be small. By the time you get into a position where major turns are necessary, you're in trouble.

6 If you started backing up straight toward the ramp, you should be able to fix any major mistakes by going forward and starting over again.

7 If you begin making corrections while driving backward toward the ramp, make sure to glance ahead to be sure the car's "bow" isn't going to hit any obstructions.

The main problem with wheel steering is that it takes up too much space. The pedestal itself is bulky in the cockpit area. Cables, gears and quadrant mechanisms below deck also take up valuable living space.

Trailerable multihulls usually have rudders that can be either raised or removed. Designs for a collapsible rudder with a wheel steering system have been either mechanically impractical or esthetically ugly.

Sailors who have gotten used to wheel steering will need to reacclimate themselves to a tiller.

CABINS
Larger catamarans usually afford a lot more living and comfort space. Cabins can be located in each hull and across the span between the hulls. The larger the cat, the easier it is to merge the cabin between the hulls with the space within the hulls to make one huge inside living area.

Unfortunately, trailerable catamarans in the 20–30 foot range cannot provide these comforts. You will probably see small cabin spaces within each hull on smaller boats.

Today's trailerable trimarans use the main hull for living space. The amas afford no living space but can be used for storage.

Prepare for mast raising by removing securing lines and unfouling rigging.

center of the boat from bow to stern. The side of the boat to leeward of that line sinks while the windward side rises.

The same thing happens on a multihull only the distance between the centerline and the edges of the deck (each hull or ama) is a lot greater. When the force that sinks the leeward side of a monohull tries to do the same to a multi, it is resisted by a very buoyant hull/ama. A combination of buoyancy and the wider beam keeps the boat upright. In addition, when the multihull begins to heel, the weight of the windward hull helps limit heeling. It takes a lot of wind to raise a hull off the water. Thus, multihulls substitute their breadth, or beam for the monohull's heavy keel. Multi–hullers sometimes refer to monohulls as "lead mines."

So, multihulls ride very flat in the water in normal winds. When the winds pick up, the monohull will heel badly, telling you to reduce sail. Not so with the multihull. The boat will continue to sail flat and go much faster.

The multihull resists heeling high up into the scale of winds, and when it finally reaches the point where there is too much wind, the boat might just go over. That is why the multihull sailor should think about reducing sail long before it becomes a danger.

A cap shroud tensioner attached to the aft portion of the ama maintains shroud tension. Roller furling boom in use (right).

Airtight compartments within the amas also ensure flotation. The Corsair F–27 tri, for example, has a cabin aft in the main hull and a V berth forward. The main salon lies in between. Living space isn't palatial, but when you add up all the boat's features, it would be hard to imagine doing more with a 27 foot boat.

STABILITY

One thing that draws more and more people to multi-hulls is their stability, with little or no heeling. They are designed that way. Monohulls use heavy, weighted keels suspended below the hull to keep the boat upright.

In theory, no matter how much you tip the boat above the waterline, gravity will not let that keel come out of the water. When a monohull heels, you can almost see a pivot line running down the

In other words, multihulls are very stable, but they do not tend to tell the sailor when they are overpowered. Chapter 3 looks at this topic in more detail.

The multihull sailor should always be on the lookout for storm clouds or other signs of adverse weather. Since the boat won't tell you when to shorten sail, you have to be vigilant in assessing the wind strength. And do not hesitate to shorten sail.

SEE APPENDIX A FOR SAILING KNOWLEDGE QUIZ

SAILING SKILLS

Now that we have had a chance to look around and learn a little about the layout and characteristics of multihulls, it's time to get the boat in the water and let it do what it does best – sail. This whole first section looks at a revolutionary and evolving type of boat that provides the advantages of other multihulls, yet can be hauled on a trailer and stored in your driveway. These features appeal to people who want to sail on bodies of water more easily accessed by

highway than waterway. Others are drawn to trailerable multis because they prefer not to pay high slip and mooring fees. While they may be the envy of their fellow boaters, there is a price to pay for versatility and thrift. It's all a matter of choice, and if you've chosen trailerable multihull sailing here's what you will need to know about launching and rigging your boat.

GETTING IT IN THE WATER

Under normal circumstances it's hardly necessary to concentrate on what's happening 20 or 30 feet in the air. In fact, unless there's something to attract our attention upward, such as a plane or a bird, we tend to look straight ahead.

This practice can be dangerous, however, for sailors who trailer boats to and from the waterfront. If electrical powerlines make contact with your mast the results can be disastrous. Make sure there are no powerlines that the mast can touch while being

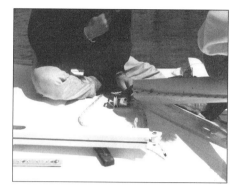

(clockwise from above) 1. Attaching mast to mast step 2. Boom used as raising device 3. Rig during raising process 4. Securing shrouds

THE PHOTOGRAPHS ABOVE ILLUSTRATE RAISING A MAST WHICH STARTS OUT TIPPED FORWARD. THESE INSTRUCTIONS REFER TO RAISING A MAST TIPPED AFT WHILE THE BOAT IS ON THE TRAILER. MOST OF THE SKILLS ARE THE SAME BUT MAY NEED TO BE ADAPTED FOR YOUR BOAT.

1 Remove the tie–downs and lights.

2 Undo the trailer winch hook, pull some slack, pass it over the bow roller, and lay it on the foredeck.

3 Place the mast–raising pole on the foredeck ready for use.

4 Get onto the bow and move aft alongside the mast, undoing the rope mast ties and rigging ties as you go.

5 Lift the forward end of the mast and walk aft, rolling the mast on the aft mast roller. You may need to stop about halfway back, rest the mast step on the deck, and go aft to lift the intermediate shrouds outside the aft mast support side tubes. Clear any other possible obstructions to the mast back until the mast step reaches the pivot brackets.

6 Now is the time to fit any masthead hardware, such as wind indicators, etc. Let the masthead dip down to the crew on the ground.

7 The mast should now be connected to the mast step.

8 Position the mast–raising pole on the mast. Then take the trailer winch hook, pull it back over the pole or bar, and connect to the jib halyard snapshackle.

raised or while backing to the launching ramp. Even getting near a line could cause an electrical arc to jump to your mast.

BACKING THE TRAILER

On close examination, driving a semi or tractor trailer truck over open roads isn't as challenging as maneuvering the big rig in tight spaces. Perhaps the most difficult part of the whole process is getting that long trailer to go backward while steering it from

Don't launch your boat without a line secured to some part of the hull.

Typical mechanical trailer winch

Check to see that the jib halyard is SECURELY TIED OFF.

9 Fit the mast raising wire or shrouds to the amas, whichever is required. Begin winching the mast up. AGAIN CHECK FOR OVERHEAD POWERLINES! As you are winching up the mast, keep checking to ensure none of the rigging snags.

10 After the mast is fully raised, connect the forestay (and babystay on some boats) to the chainplate.

11 After the stays are all con-nected slack off on the trailer winch and disconnect the jib halyard.

12 Thread the running rigging through all the blocks and clutches required for operation.

13 Mount the booms and sail.

14 Remove the mast pole and stow.

LAUNCHING:

1 Back the trailer down the ramp until it is submerged. Refer to the manufacturer's instruc-tions for specifics on submerging

the trailer. Generally, on small-er boats you can stop before the wheel bearings submerge which will keep them healthy longer.

2 Attach a bow line.

3 As soon as the engine is in the water, be sure to start the engine and get it warmed up before casting the boat off.

4 After you have warmed up the engine, disconnect the winch hook and push the boat off.

One of the most appealing features of a folding trimaran is its ability to fit into a standard slip. (Top) A winch is used to unfold an ama. (Bottom)

turns. The boat could roll over. You might want to get at least one ama extended in this case.

UNFOLDING A TRIMARAN

Before unfolding a trimaran check that there are no ropes across the beam recesses and that the tiller is clear.

1 Remove the beam locking pins.
2 Place your foot on the top of the upper folding strut.

3 Grasp the top of the beam and pull downward, while pushing with your foot.

CAUTION: Always make sure no one has his foot/hand/fingers in or near the beam recesses as the beams can come down quickly.

The ama will unfold, but be sure it doesn't pick up too much speed toward the end of its extension. Don't let it bang down.

Hold the beam down and tighten the bolts with a speed wrench. They should be tightened firmly, but do not overtighten. Beam bolts should all be in place and tightened before sailing.

Some boats have swing amas instead of folding amas. These swing forward and are secured with a locking cable or strut in similar fashion.

At this point on some trimarans you will need to attach the upper shrouds to the chainplates on the amas. Then tension the shrouds for sailing. Sight up the mast to ensure it is in column, which should be the case after equally tightening the lower shrouds. Then tighten the upper shrouds moderately, using the same tension on both sides. Sight up the mast once again and adjust uppers and/or lowers on either side to get the mast straight. Don't forget to replace cotter pins or keys after tightening turnbuckles.

inside the tractor.

Backing up a boat trailer with a car or pick–up is much easier than the same move with a semi, but the concepts are the same. If you haven't done it before, plan on practice and patience. And don't schedule your practice on a launch ramp during a busy, summer afternoon. If you do, you may find your normally friendly fellow boaters turning to scurvy, mutinous pirates. The best place to acquire these skills is in an open area such as a parking lot on a light traffic day.

Trailering skills are no different from sailing skills. They improve with practice.

MAST STEPPING

With the centerboard or daggerboard up, the boat will be hard to handle in any crosswinds, so make it a priority to get a board down at the first opportunity. Folding trimarans can be quite unstable with their amas folded, so watch out for crosswinds and sharp

CHAPTER 2
GETTING STARTED

SAILING KNOWLEDGE

"It would give the most skillful [European] builder a shock to see craft having no more breadth of beam than three [arm] spans carrying a spread of sail so large as to befit one of ours with a beam of eight or ten spans, and which, though without means of lowering or furling the sail, make sport of the winds and waves during a gale, their safety depending wholly on two light poles a couple of varas of so long (about eight feet), which, being placed athwartships, the one forward and the other aft, are fitted to another spar of soft wood placed fore and aft wise in the manner of an outrigger."

Corney
–Andia y Varela

Multihulls are often seen as novelty vessels but an old story puts that in perspective rather humorously:

What if America had been discovered by the Polynesians, rather than Scandinavians? Well, we'd all be sailing multihulls. Then someone would come along and say, "Hey, I have a great idea. I'm going to design a boat with just one hull."

Everyone would ask how it would keep itself upright and Mr. Monohull would reply, "Weights and a deep keel. I'll put a lot of weight down deep in the water."

Then everyone would ask if that wouldn't make the boat go very slow, and he would enthusiastically reply, "Yes! Yes! YES!" You can bet slow and heavy would soon have advocates and a new novelty would be born.

Speed, more than any other factor, sets multihulls apart

from most sailboats on the water. Quickness of vessels with multiple hulls comes from their power to weight ratio. In other words, they have a lot of sail power and relatively little weight. Chapter 1 discusses how wider beams and flotation in hulls and amas keep multihulls sailing flat in conditions where monohulls would heel. These construction and design fac-

tors eliminate the need for heavy keels making the vessel much lighter.

Without the need for more buoyancy to keep all that extra monohull keel weight afloat, hulls on multis can be thinner and sleeker. Boats with thinner, sleeker hulls go faster by displacing less water.

Imagine taking a monohull and placing it in a huge vat of Jell–O. If you pulled it out, the shape of the hull from waterline to keel would remain (at least in our imaginations). If you filled that indentation, shaped exactly like our sailboat hull, with water, you would have the volume of water the hull displaces, or the "hull's displacement."

Create another indentation just forward of the original one using the same method. When the boat moves from the first position to the second position, it has to move the amount of water it took to fill the first indentation.

Float the hull or ama from a comparable length multi-

This displacement mono-hull (above) gets its buoy-ancy from its broad under-water surface. A typical trimaran with raised stern sections (left). This hatch (below) gives you access to the ama and should help keep water out.

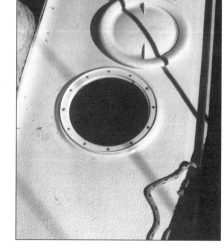

hull in the same vat of Jell–O and it would take much less water to fill the indentation. Therefore, moving from one position to the next displaces less water and takes less energy.

Buoyant hulls have to be fat. They displace more water and consequently need more energy to make them move. So, all that monohull keel weight requires a fatter, slower hull.

Multihulls, on the other hand, are lighter and require a lot less buoyancy. So, they can have thinner hulls, displace less water and usually move faster.

STOWAGE ABOARD

First of all, keep in mind that weight increases displacement and slows the overall performance of any cat or tri. Any weight you do bring aboard should be prudent-ly distributed to avoid uneven weight concentration. You would not want to put all your gear in one hull on a catamaran or one ama on a trimaran. Your boat would list to one side and perfor-mance would be thrown out of whack.

When one hull or ama carries more weight or the bow or stern of a hull or ama is more heavily loaded, the boat's hydrody-namic design features will fail. You would not want to place heavy loads forward in the boat. If the wind picks up, you will discov-er that the bows tend to dig deeper and deeper into the water. Some modern multihulls address this problem through design features that work against this tendency, but you still don't want to encour-age dipping bows.

To counteract dipping of the bows, you want as much weight aft as possible. On the other hand, if you are going for speed in light air, you want the weight forward. In cruising, safety is king, so think aft for stowage.

All smaller multihulls suf-fer from poverty of stowage space. On trimarans, the amas usually have access hatches where things can be stored. These spaces easily accommodate such things as fend-ers, lines, and other equipment that can tolerate a little water. Do not load heavy material in one ama and light material in the other – again, you want to keep the boat balanced.

A Closer Look
Cockpit & Deck Area

On smaller multihull cruiser/racers, space restrictions will not permit a winch for every halyard and sheet. Additional winches also add unwanted weight.

So, you may have many sheets and halyards set up to feed one winch. Most control lines led to a single winch will go through a stopper or clutch. These line–holding devices allow a sheet or halyard to be winched to where you want it set. Then the stopper is locked to keep it there, thus freeing the winch for another use.

More lines led to one winch means more chances for tangling. Some multihulls will place a sheet bag on a bulkhead or elsewhere in the cockpit. Be sure to carefully coil lines after use and place them neatly in the sheet bag or on deck. Separate any line and re–coil it before releasing it and letting it run.

A control line that has any noticeable load on it when it sits in a stopper should be released carefully using the following steps:

1 Unfoul and coil the line.

2 Clear the winch if another line has been left on it.

3 Take two wraps around the winch with the line to be released.

4 Grind the winch, just enough to transfer the load from the stopper to the winch.

5 Release the stopper.

6 Ease the line back from the winch being careful not to let your hands get pulled into the winch.

The first thing you will notice about a catamaran or trimaran is the expansive room on

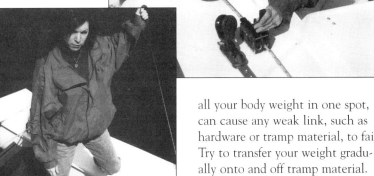

(Clockwise from above) 1. The stopper/clutch holds this line when it is removed from the winch. 2. Lines released from a stopper/clutch should be coiled and ready to run. 3. Always transfer a load to a winch or cleat before releasing a stopper/clutch. 4. Don't expect a solid surface when you step onto trampoline material.

deck. In many cases, most of the deck is just netting. Netting is used to save weight, thus allowing the boat to develop more speed. Folding a multihull is also made much easier through the use of netting, and it's a great surface for messy jobs like cleaning fish and washing dishes. A free flow of water cleans any debris that may be left behind.

Learning to navigate the deck of a trailerable multihull requires coming to terms with the netting or trampoline (tramp) material. Use your own flexibility to propel your body from one step to the next. A stiff leg, focusing all your body weight in one spot, can cause any weak link, such as hardware or tramp material, to fail. Try to transfer your weight gradually onto and off tramp material.

Sailplans

Since the boat is light and its speed through the water is not as restricted as a monohull, a wider selection of sails can be used.

Rigs

Most multihulls use a fractional sloop rig in which the headstay attaches to the mast below the masthead. The masthead sloop whose headstay attach-

A fractional rig will have its forestay attached to the mast somewhere below the masthead.

A high–aspect ratio mainsail

es to the top of the mast has lost popularity, and hardly any boats use split rigs (yawls or ketches) and cutters.

THE MAINSAIL

Most modern multihulls use a high–aspect–ratio mainsail. This means that the measurement at the foot (width) of the sail is less than normal, while the measurement of the luff (height) of the sail is greater than normal. The result is a taller, slimmer–looking sail. Aspect ratio simply refers to the relative measurements of height and width.

Leeches of most conventional mainsails are pretty much a straight line from the top of the mast to the aft part of the boom. A roach is added material extending beyond that line. The added material is supported by battens. In

most cases, multihulls use full–length battens and their mainsails normally carry a lot of roach. This allows them to take advantage of the more powerful winds higher above the water's surface.

Full–length battens not only

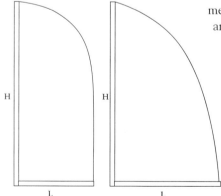

The shorter boom on the left sail would be an example of high–aspect ratio.

support the extra roach material, they also hold sail shape in the body of the mainsail in all conditions. A fully battened main often has a mind of its own during sail raising and lowering. It may be difficult getting it up, but the thing it wants to do most is sail.

The square–headed mainsail has been used on multihulls with favorable results. This not only creates a lot of roach, but it begins the roach system from the top of the mast. It extends straight back for quite a distance, and then squares off and continues the roachy leech to the boom. The square head is held out by battens.

In light air it allows for a lot more power at the top of the sail where it can do the most good. When a puff of wind hits the top of the sail, the long arm of the roach up top blows off away from the wind. Sail area is automatically reduced at the top of the mast. This phenomenon lowers the geometric center of power of the sail, which reduces heeling. When the puff goes away, the top of the sail returns to where it was and the power returns. And, if the wind increases steadily, you simply haul in only the mainsheet and the top again blows off.

Let's talk a bit about the "Power Button." If we were to measure the mainsail geometrically and find the exact center, we could say that is where the power is concentrated – The Power Button.

We want the button high in lighter winds. A small amount of force will have more effect concentrated at the top of the mast than it will dispersed at the bottom of the mast.

Here's why. If

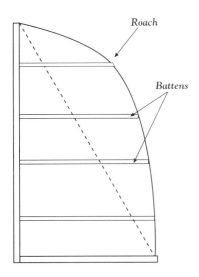

The roach on this sail extends quite a bit beyond the line drawn between head and clew. Full battens are necessary to give it shape.

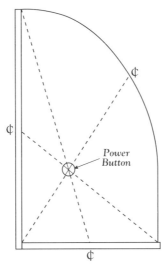

Simply finding the center of a triangle formed by the foot, leech and luff doesn't take all the material in the roach into consideration. However, this simple method will suffice for the sake of our discussion.

you push a sailboat's mast in any direction, the boat will move away from the force. Watch the mast on a rolling or pitching sailboat. The top of the mast moves much further than lower sections each time the boat rocks. Therefore, we can say the same amount of force that moves the bottom of the mast 1 foot, moves the top 4 feet (these numbers are used only as an example). In this example, moving the top of the mast one foot would take 1/4 the force necessary to move the bottom of the mast the same distance. Therefore, if you only have a small force, concentrating it at the top of the mast will produce best results.

When the wind picks up, we don't want that button up high anymore. It will cause the boat to heel more and sink the leeward hull or ama, reducing speed through the water. We use the downhaul to lower the button.

Downhauling makes the mast bend, which flattens the sail. The top of the sail and upper leech blow off to leeward. This renders the top part of the sail useless (almost like reefing the sail). It also lowers our power button and

reduces the tendency of the boat to heel. It's worth taking time to perfect mainsail trim. The mainsail is your sailplan's main engine on a multihull.

HEADSAILS

Most boats start off with a genoa in lighter air. The genoa overlaps the mainsail, whereas a jib does not overlap. The genoa is more difficult to handle during tacks and jibes but the additional sail area optimizes power in lighter winds.

The fully battened jib, an idea the Hobie Cat Company came up with years ago, has been rejuvenated in cruising/racing multihulls. By making the jib fully battened, the sail maintains an almost solid, wing-like shape. The consistent shape draws wind more efficiently across the leeward side of the mainsail. This gives you the easy handling ability of the smaller jib, plus the power and pointing ability of a genoa. Many boats now use a screacher.

The name comes loosely from what the sail is, a combination spinnaker and reacher. For ease of operation, this overly large, genoa–type sail uses a roller furler. The tack of the sail mounts on a bowsprit that extends well past the bow of the boat. Obviously, this sail should only be used in lighter winds. Some experts claim that it should not be used in winds over 10–12 mph.

On a close reach, the screacher can be used with a jib. This adds sail area and an additional slot. Expect a lot more speed.

Keep in mind that headsails add more wind speed and pressure to the leeward side of sails behind them. That means the screacher is helping the jib, and the jib is helping the mainsail. With all this help the boat is going to go a lot faster.

Spinnakers can be symmetrical or asymmetrical. Most monohulls use symmetrical spinnakers. They are designed to be used more or less like a barndoor – adding sail area to help the boat sail downwind.

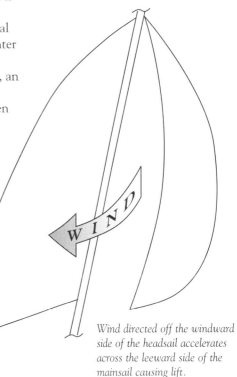

Wind directed off the windward side of the headsail accelerates across the leeward side of the mainsail causing lift.

This trimaran mainsheet/traveler spans the cockpit just like it would on a similar sized monohull.

Asymmetric spinnakers, on the other hand, are built like huge, very full, heavy–shouldered genoas.

Asymmetric spinnakers are usually tacked onto a bowsprit set well forward of the bow, and trimmed to the leeward side. The boat does not sail straight downwind, but rather on a broad–reaching angle. Quite often, a jib can be flown between the spinnaker and the mainsail for more speed. In lighter winds however, the jib insert is not very effective and sometimes prevents wind from fully inflating the spinnaker.

MAINSHEETS

Mainsheets are the sailing throttle of multihulls. They can aid driving and steering the boat more effectively than any other sail control.

The mainsheet has little mystery about it. It trims the mainsail. But multihulls with high–aspect mainsails require a lot more power to pull down on the leech of the sail. It's all a matter of leverage.

A see–saw is probably the most universally familiar application of leverage. The closer you get to the pivot point (fulcrum) of a see–saw, the harder it is to get someone up in the air that's sitting on the other end. Sometimes two people sitting near the fulcrum can't lift one person their own size at the other end.

The same thing happens with a mainsail. The boom pivots at the gooseneck. The closer you are to the gooseneck, the harder it will be to pull down on the sail. A high aspect ratio mainsail has a short boom which means it takes more power than a longer boom would take to pull it down.

Most mainsheets are pretty easy to figure out – simply grab the sheet at the cleat and pull. Cleat it when it's sheeted properly. But multihulls tend to have more sophisticated sheeting systems.

In one case, the sheeting block has two cleats. If you want to pull in the sail at a 4:1 ratio, which would be very quick but without much power, you would grab both sheets coming out of both cleats and pull.

If you want to sheet the sail tighter with an 8:1 ratio, which is slower hauling but twice as powerful, you simply drop one of the sheets from one of the cleats (leaving it cleated) and pull on the sheet from the other cleat.

Still another system uses a cascading mechanism. That is, if you have a 6:1 ratio mainsheet, and then attach a separate 4:1 ration system to the end of that, you will not end up with 10:1, you get a 24:1 ratio – cascading multiplies rather than adds to ratio. In this case, you would pull from the 6:1 cleats to bring the

sail in quickly, but with little power. Once the main was as tight as you could get it with the 6:1 system, you would pull from the cleat with the cascading sheet to further tighten the sail. With the 24:1 ratio, you would be pulling in more slowly, yet with much more power.

Monohull sailors who aren't concerned about performance can cleat the mainsheet and leave it unattended for hours at a time, even in freshening breezes.

Not so with multihulls. The mainsheet will be the first defense against winds that can threaten to capsize a multihull. For this reason, multihull sailors rarely ignore the mainsheet.

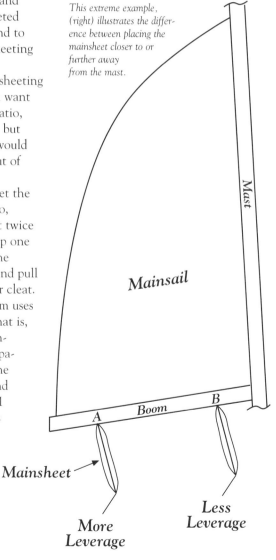

This extreme example, (right) illustrates the difference between placing the mainsheet closer to or further away from the mast.

MAINSHEET TRAVELERS

Travelers alter the position where a mainsheet attaches to the hull. Most sailors pay closest attention to travelers going to weather. In heavier winds the traveler is set on the boat's centerline, causing the mainsheet to pull directly down and flatten the mainsail.

As winds lighten the traveler moves to weather and the sheet is eased. The resulting angle allows the sail to twist off to leeward for maximum performance. Some performance multihull sailors have begun to favor using the traveler to force the boom slightly to windward in light air. The sail still twists but the leech stays closer to the centerline. Special double traveler systems may be used to achieve this sail trim.

OUTHAULS

There are two ways to sheet the mainsail – pulling down on a conventional boom to tighten the sail, or by pulling on the clew of the sail, as is done with a boomless rig. We may begin seeing more production boats using boomless rigs. They give you control of the mainsail comparable to that achieved with a boom while saving a lot of weight and removing the danger of concussion from a boom.

The outhaul is set tight most of the time, except when sailing off the wind. Tightening it pulls the foot of the sail taut along the boom. For boomless rigs, the same effect is achieved by moving the traveler car on the clew of the sail forward, or by moving the clew hook forward. You want the bottom of the sail flat since this is the area that the jib or genoa overlaps. If the mainsail is too full near the bottom, the jib will backwind it.

By spanning nearly the entire width of this trimaran cockpit, this traveler maximizes sail trimming options.

Some boomless rigs allow for such accurate sail trim, sailors wonder why they needed one in the first place.

Backwinding the mainsail makes for slow sailing.

When sailing off the wind, the outhaul can be released. For boomless rigs, the traveler car would move aft on the sail clew, or the clew hook would be in the outer hole. This easing of the foot of the sail allows the sail to get fuller and therefore more powerful. Off the wind the jib or genoa is also way out. So, you need not worry about backwinding the mainsail.

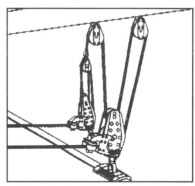

Adding a 6:1 to a 4:1 creates a cascading system which giveproduces 24:1 purchase.

JIB SHEETS

Jib sheets attach to the clew of the headsail. They run back through a turning block that sets the angle of the sheet, allowing the sail to be trimmed with minimum resistance. Turning blocks also allow the sheet to feed properly onto the winch.

JIB AND SCREACHER SHEET TRACKS

Many boats have fairlead tracks that can quickly change the angle at which a jib sheet attaches to a clew. Move the car forward on the track and leech tension increases while foot tension is reduced. Moving the car aft creates the opposite reaction. These adjustments are usually controlled from the cockpit. Always ease sheets before adjusting. The procedure will become much less difficult and the potential for injury and damage will be reduced.

On most trailerable multis, the track is located atop the cabin and can only be trimmed fore and aft. The track is typically fitted with a roller–bearing car. Adjustments in and out are done with the use of a barberhauler (we will talk about that in a moment).

If you set the jib lead forward, pulling down heavily on the leech and lightly on the foot of the sail, a much fuller jib will result. While fullness normally increases power, this particular setting will not help the overall sailplan. You don't want a tight leech. When you pull down hard on the leech the wind is hooked back into the mainsail (remember, the main engine on multihulls). Again, this is backwinding and backwinding destroys the airflow across the backside of the mainsail and consequently destroys the speed of the boat.

Setting the leads too far aft pulls the foot tight and only puts a light pull on the leech. The consequence is a flatter sail, with a leech that will open up or blow off to leeward too much. While it is a good idea to have the leech open somewhat, to avoid backwinding the mainsail, it is not a good idea to have it blow way out. You need the jib to help blow air rapidly across the backside of the mainsail to increase your power.

Ideally, you want the jib lead pulling a little harder back on the foot of the sail than down on the leech.

SPINNAKER SHEETS AND GUYS

These sheets control the large headsails used while sailing off the wind. They usually attach to a block located as far aft and outboard as possible. A turning block is usually used to lead the sheet back to a winch.

While spinnaker rigging and flying require their own specialized training, it is important for you to recognize spinnaker gear when you board a multihull.

BARBERHAULERS

Another jib adjustment used primarily by racers is the barberhauler. It allows the fairlead to be adjusted inboard and outboard.

In light winds an eased outhaul (above) on a fully battened mainsail doesn't cause dramatic changes in sail trim. This jibsheet is lead directly across the trimaran's cabin top.

Barberhaulers usually consist of a short length of line with a hook on one end. The hook attaches to the clew and the end of the line runs outboard (or possibly inboard) to a block, then, possibly, through a turning block to a winch. The barberhauler usually runs perpendicular to, or at a slight angle pulling back on, the jib sheet. Adjusting tension on both the barberhauler and the sheet allows the clew to move inboard and outboard. This opens and closes the slot between the mainsail and jib, allowing for optimum air flow between the sails.

DOWNHAUL OR CUNNINGHAM

These two terms have become nearly synonymous. Smaller boats can use a single line (downhaul) while larger vessels use a block–and–tackle system (cunningham). Either way, they pull down on the luff of the mainsail. In the case of downhauls, they actually pull the boom down.

In general, downhauls, cunninghams and other mainsail flattening adjustments should be applied as the wind increases and eased as the wind dies down.

MARKING SHEETS

Did you ever wonder how violin players know exactly where to put their fingers without frets marked off the way they are on a guitar neck? It comes with practice which may account for how awful beginning violinists usually sound.

A similar principle applies to sail trim. You can choose to figure it out again every time you sail, or you can create premarked "frets" like the guitar neck.

When you get things set pretty well going to weather, mark all the sheets with laundry marker pen, or Plasticote Autographics

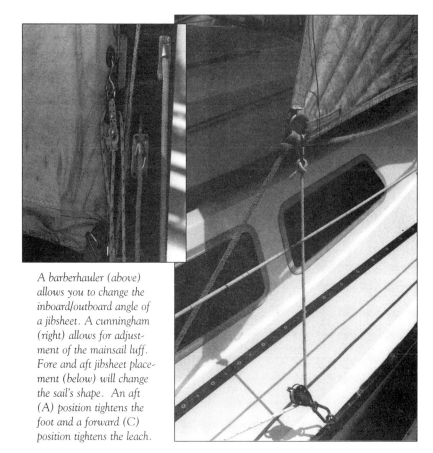

A barberhauler (above) allows you to change the inboard/outboard angle of a jibsheet. A cunningham (right) allows for adjustment of the mainsail luff. Fore and aft jibsheet placement (below) will change the sail's shape. An aft (A) position tightens the foot and a forward (C) position tightens the leach.

Pen. You can set the mark at a block or beside some part of the boat over which the sheet passes. Just remember which bolt head or stripe is the spot that determines sail trim.

Marking will give you a ballpark, rule-of-thumb setting that will get you sailing pretty close to maximum speed as quickly as possible. You can do the same thing on other points of sail as well.

DAGGERBOARD AND CENTERBOARDS

Dinghy sailors are quite familiar with the concept of retractable centerboards and daggerboards. They are pushed down through the hull so that they protrude into the water. Whenever a multihull

C

B

A

Adjustable Fairlead Track

A

B

C

that has boards gets pushed sideways, the centerboard or daggerboard resists that leeway just like a ballasted keel. Boards also provide a pivot point for turning.

Most sailors discover that lift, similar to lift experienced by sails, also occurs on underwater appendages – the boards and rudders. Keels and rudders are shaped thicker toward the leading edge and thinner aft. Water follows this uneven contour and lifts the side that would be windward while propelling the boat forward.

In multihulls, hull shape below the water performs these same tasks. You can see this distinctly on some beach cats. The outside surface of the hull will be almost flat while the inside edge is curved to promote lift.

Daggerboards and centerboards can be pulled up when underwater lift is not needed. Big, metal keels don't lift in this manner. Daggerboard and centerboard multihulls have the ability to get into very shallow water with their boards up. This is great for launching, beaching, or getting into secluded gunkholes.

SEE APPENDIX A FOR SAILING KNOWLEDGE QUIZ

This daggerboard trunk (top) illustrates the asymmetrical nature of this underwater appendage. The small knob on top of the filler cap (above) is the air vent.

SAILING SKILLS

ENGINE STARTING

Weight consciousness dictates that most small multihulls use outboard engines rather than heavier inboard diesels. Trimarans usually have an outboard well in which the engine is mounted. Remote controls are mounted somewhere in the cockpit for ease of operation. Others simply hang the engine off a mount somewhere on the stern.

Standing in the cockpit, locate the engine. Is it in a well, or hung off the stern?

Once the engine has started, allow it to warm up a few minutes before casting off. Cold engines like to quit without any warning.

PROPELLER FORCES

Prop–walk is a tendency for propellers to pull a boat's stern in a lateral direction. Imagine the prop as a rubber tire touching the bottom of the waterway. If the prop is turning clockwise or to the right, the rubber wheel will try to move the stern of the boat to the right. If it turns counterclockwise or to the left, the rubber wheel will try to move the stern to the left. As long as you know which direction, clockwise (called right–handed) or counterclockwise (called left–handed), the prop turns in forward, the image of a tire will help you anticipate prop–walk. While this pulling of the stern happens all the time, it is most noticeable in reverse.

Outboard engines have prop–walk tendencies, but not nearly as much as fixed–prop boats with inboard engines. Less powerful engines and propellers designed for maximum forward thrust account for the difference.

Turning the outboard engine turns the direction of its thrust and may be possible on some trailerable multihulls. Stern–mounted engines usually have this capability.

If you want to turn hard to the left, the rudder alone will

Trimaran at rest with its daggerboards retracted.

turn the boat as long as you are moving relatively fast. Water volume against the rudder, concentrated by speed through the water, will have a dramatic effect on your turn. However, as the speed decreases, less water contacts the turned rudder and the boat turns in a wider arc.

Normally, an outboard engine faces directly forward to ensure its force pushes the boat ahead with maximum efficiency. By turning the motor, you can direct the force to one side or the other and cause the boat to turn much more sharply.

The same reduction in turning radius would occur when

A propeller turning to the right will tend to pull the stern to the right. The same thing happens in the reverse direction. Make sure you know whether your prop turns left or right in forward or reverse.

using reverse power. If the skipper wanted the stern to go to port, he would simply turn the engine hard right (the outboard handle works just like a tiller) and reverse the engine.

Most boats with well–mounted engines, on the other hand, will not have ample

room to turn the engine within the well. They will have to rely on prop–walk to help maneuver the boat. Keep in mind that prop–walk will not be as strong as it is with fixed–prop inboards.

EVERY OUTBOARD ENGINE HAS ITS OWN STARTING INSTRUCTIONS AND THEY SHOULD BE READ CAREFULLY. HERE'S A TYPICAL OUTBOARD MOTOR STARTING PROCEDURE.

1 Check to be sure the fuel line is connected and that you have an adequate amount of fuel in the tank.

2 Open vent on top of the tank filler or the tank itself.

3 Pump the rubber, in–line bulb to get gas into the carburetor. Stop when the gas bulb gets firm and you cannot feel any more gas moving through it.

4 Be sure the water intake is in the water. You can find the water intake by looking for slots or grills along the leading edge of the propeller shaft. Most engines have an outlet that spurts a steady little squirt of water. You know the engine is getting water for cooling purposes when you see this stream.

5 Most engines have a primer or choke. This should

be used for cold–starting. Look for some kind of readily available lever or handle that is pulled, pushed or twisted. The choke can be turned off gradually as the engine begins to warm up. An engine that needs choke to keep from stalling after it has warmed up should be brought in for service.

6 Check for a switch, key or emergency shut–off key and put it in the "on" position.

7 Set the throttle to "start."

8 Pull the starter cord or turn the starter switch until the engine comes to life.

9 Turn the choke off gradually until the engine can run without it.

(left to right) 1. Pumping bowl to prime carburetor. 2. Pull the curly cord on this engine and it will shut down. 3. Placing your idle hand on top of the engine while starting will help avoid losing balance.

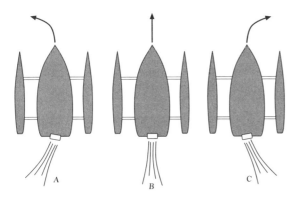

Directing the outboard's thrust to port (A) turns the bow to port. Straight ahead (B) pushes it straight and starboard thrust (C) turns the bow to starboard.

LEAVING A DOCK

If you have a folding–type multihull, you will find that dockage is more easily available when the boat is in the folded position. They are designed to fit into a standard slip in that configuration.

When leaving the dock you should be cautious of the wind. In the folded position, the boat presents a very large surface for the wind to push around. If there is a crosswind, where the wind hits the boat somewhat across the beam, it can dramatically affect boat handling.

Use of a running spring line will help keep the boat going in the right direction. Lines used in knot tying or boat operations are often said to have two ends, a running end and a standing end. The standing end is stationary or otherwise tied to something. The running end does the work. A running spring line is simply a dock line that has no knots, particularly at the running end.

On folding multihulls the amas should be unfolded as soon as possible – in the folded position the boat can be pretty unstable in crosswinds or during quick turns. It could roll over. So, let's do that now.

WARNING: Watch that your fingers or toes do not get caught while unfolding the amas.

Now that the amas are out and tightened down, the boat is much more stable and we no longer have to worry about getting into crosswinds or currents that could cause problems.

MANEUVERING

First, let's throw a marker consisting of a float and some sort of anchor attached by a line, into the water. A fixed marker with plenty of open water on all sides would work just as well.

Now, let's attempt to stop the boat within four feet of the marker. It's important to know all your boat's capabilities, including what it takes to bring it to a stop.

You will probably find that the boat maneuvers much eas-

Stopping a trailerable multihull upwind under power will allow for more control, at least until it is completely stopped.

ier with the centerboard or dagger-board(s) down. This gives the boat an axis on which to turn.

First try it the easy way by bringing the boat to a stop with the bow into the wind. It will require much less reverse engine thrust to stop. However, approach slowly even with this knowledge. The bow will want to blow off to either side, so the helmsman must use thrust and steering to compensate. If the bow starts to drift to the right, put the helm over to starboard to turn the bow back to the left. If you have no way (forward motion), the rudder will not help at all. It's the same as turning the wheels of your car when it's stopped: nothing happens.

As mentioned previously, the engine's thrust will help you turn when the rudder loses control. If you have an engine that moves, try turning it to compensate for the wind's effects. It's a great exercise to help you get used to working with wind and current.

If your engine cannot be

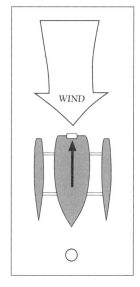

Backing into the wind is the "path of least resistance" when motoring in reverse.

called upon to help you, try using minimum forward motion and turn the rudder to keep the bows into the wind. If the current is running the same direction as the wind, and if you can set the motor to a speed about the same as the current, you will stay in one place relative to the marker. If you can master these moves without going crazy, you're on your way to becoming a multihull expert.

The down-wind course calls for an even slower approach, since it will take much more reverse thrust to stop the boat. So, start early with reverse thrust and be ready to apply additional

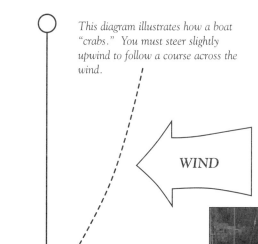

This diagram illustrates how a boat "crabs." You must steer slightly upwind to follow a course across the wind.

When the boat has cleared the slip bow crew releases the running end of the dockline and pulls the line aboard.

power. Holding the bow straight downwind is much easier than holding the bow into the wind. Here the wind helps keep the stern into it without blowing the bow to either side.

You want to approach very slowly, and at two or three boat lengths from the mark, try reverse. Notice that it doesn't slow the boat very much. Add more reverse power until you can see that it will stop. Now you are probably about a boat length away. Allow the boat to drift downwind a little more by backing off on the throttle. Increase speed to stop your downwind motion.

For crosswind approaches, you will notice that you have to make a crab–like approach to the mark. The crab reference comes from the way crabs move forward by walking sideways. Your bow

Backing against tension on this running spring line helps fight the effects of a crosswind.

angles upwind of the mark rather than pointing directly at it. The amount of angle depends on the wind velocity; more wind, more upwind angle. The idea is to equalize the distance to leeward you will be pushed (due to wind) with the distance you steer to windward. The boat's course to the mark should be perpendicular to the wind despite the fact that it is pointing upwind. It's an inexact science, but you can make adjustments by watching your boat's approach to the mark and altering your helm angle as needed.

Use reverse and possibly some rudder to stop the boat. Once stopped, the bow will not remain where you pointed it – the wind will quickly blow it downwind.

Next, let's try motoring across the wind and/or current slowly. First, do it with the boards up. Notice that the heading you took (let's assume you were heading for a green daymark) will not get you to your destination. To get to the destination, you will have

to head the bow higher into the wind, as we did in the previous exercise.

Try the same thing again with the boards down. This time you will notice you still have to crab but not nearly as much. By the way, in both cases, the higher the speed across the wind and/or current the less crabbing you will have to do.

Caution: It is normally not safe to motor in heavy crosswinds with a folded multihull.

As an interesting aside here, how would you know you are in a crosswind or cross current? If you are in fairly close proximity to land, a good way to discover this is by using a transit or a range. As we saw when we were heading for that green daymark, we knew there was wind across the beam so we point-

Steering a straight course against almost any kind of crosswind will usually land you somewhere downwind.

WIND

ed the bow above the mark to actually get there. But, if you just pointed your bow at the mark and steered a straight course, you would end up downwind or downcurrent and miss the mark. If it had been a channel you needed to stay in, you would probably have gone aground.

Avoid problems by picking out a stationary object behind the green daymark. Sighting the line on which the two objects lie is

Mariners line up the dark stripes on these signs above one another to tell them they are on a predetermined course called a range.

Traveling fast in reverse makes steering and overall boat control extremely challenging.

Turning radius under power or sail is significantly increased with boards up.

Boards
Down

Boards
Up

called a transit or range. Set yourself up on the line and try to steer to it with a neutral rudder. If you cannot stay on the line, there is either wind, current, or both pushing you off course. Try again using the method of heading into the wind and/or current described above to stay on course.

This can also be done going away from an object. The secret is to line up a stationary object behind the initial object and sight it across the stern.

Now let's see how sharply the boat will turn. First, find lots of open water and try making as tight a circle as you can with the board(s) up, engine straight. Note the radius of the turn.

Next, put the board(s) down and try again. You should see a much tighter circle for the turn. And, for an even tighter circle, turn the outboard engine the same direction as the rudder and see that the boat can almost turn in a circle within its own length.

Try the same thing in the opposite direction. Factors such as position of the engine relative to the centerline and its ability to turn in one or the other direction will have an effect on turning to port or starboard. If you determine, for example, that the boat turns much tighter to port, then you should favor that side whenever possible.

Now, try the same exercises in reverse. Expect less speed and a different turning radius. In some cases, turns could be tighter in reverse. Boats with turning engines will do much tighter turns here as well.

The next task is to back up about ten boat lengths in a straight line. Use your engine and helm. If the stern starts to kick to the left, put the tiller over to port. That will make the back edge of the rudder point to the right. With the water coming across the rudder in that manner, the stern should start coming back to the right. Try to anticipate course changes and make small corrections soon rather than large corrections later.

PERSON OVERBOARD DRILL

While motoring along, a cushion accidentally goes overboard. This is a great time to practice overboard drills.

One person should yell "Person Overboard" and point at the cushion in the water. In adverse conditions, the pointer may be the only one that can keep a bearing on the swimmer, since everyone else will be busy. If it were a real person a Type IV, personal flotation device would be thrown to the victim immediately.

The helmsman should travel just far enough away and downwind to make a sharp U–turn and head back the way the boat was traveling. Take care not to hit the person in the water by turning too soon.

It is important for the helmsperson to stay in constant communication with the pointer. When the person overboard is within view, take a heading that will allow you an approach going into the wind. Approach as if you were approaching the mark we used earlier – slowly and under complete control.

When you are on your final approach, within two or three boats lengths, test your stopping ability. Be sure you can stop before running over the victim. Try to stop the boat beside the victimized cushion and retrieve it. Make sure the engine is in neutral when you approach the victim. Once the victim is firmly controlled by the crew, turn the engine off. Learning how the boat handles in different wind and wave conditions could take some practice.

By moving away from an overboard victim skipper and crew can prepare an approach that minimizes danger and maximizes the crew's ability to assist the victim.

With a real victim this crew would probably have better luck assisting a victim onto one of the amas where the freeboard is lowest.

If this were a real person in the water, a boat hook might be the wrong choice of recovery equipment. On one hand it could help bridge the gap between the boat and victim. It might also injure the person in the water. Use a boat hook or any pole with great care and only if a line is impractical.

You need to know at least two ways to bring people aboard who may or may not be able to help themselves. You must assume an overboard victim cannot clamber aboard by him or herself.

With trimarans, the amas have very little freeboard, and a couple of crew members need only reach down and drag the person up over the ama and onto the trampoline.

One of the first things to do is to prepare a crewman to strip off most unneeded clothing, put on a PFD, and get into a harness or otherwise arrange a line to attach him/her to the boat. If the person in the water needs help, your crew member can get in the water and get to work at a moment's notice. No heroics allowed, however.

Still another way to get the person on board is to rig a sling to your mainsail halyard. Since you have been motoring, the mainsail halyard is not being used. Rig up a bridle by simply tying a bowline with a big loop (big enough to slip over a person's shoulders). When alongside the victim, have the person in the water slip the loop of the bowline over his or her head and shoulders with the knot in front. Have him or her hold onto the line and then winch the victim aboard.

APPROACHING PARALLEL TO A DOCK

Always assess the wind and/or current direction to determine which is stronger. Then make your approach with your bow into whichever is stronger. Again, always approach docks slowly – remember your engine's reverse limitations.

Before approaching make sure you have a game plan for docking. Ready the crew with coiled lines and fenders. Have two people (if possible), one at the bow and one at the stern, prepared to step onto the dock. In addition to the game plan, think about what you will do if something goes awry.

For example, if the wind should blow the bow off toward the dock too early, motoring forward could cause a pretty bad crash. Trying to put the helm over toward the dock and adding more engine thrust could also spell disaster. Most likely, the boat wouldn't turn fast enough and the added power would make for a harder crash. If the bow did happen to get back into the wind (which it probably wouldn't) then the stern might hit the dock.

In either of these cases, hard reverse thrust (turned away from the dock, if the engine can be

Running a jack line along the gunwale on this trimaran makes more sense than tying it to the bow and stern of the ama. Crew can reach the entire deck from the main hull.

rotated) and putting the helm hard over toward the dock should help you get clear. After safely maneuvering away from the dock, make another attempt. It's like riding a horse. You have to get right back on after you get knocked off.

If the bow was blown away from the dock, just go ahead and give the engine forward thrust, turn away form the dock and try again.

A large loop created by a bowline and attached to a halyard can get a victim out of the water with minimal assistance.

STOPPING THE ENGINE

Feel free to let the engine idle in neutral while the boat is being secured to its dock or mooring. Many untrained skippers turn off the engine as soon as the boat is near the dock. This takes away all of your maneuvering abilities. Stopping the engine is a simple matter of turning the switch, key or emergency shut–off key to the off position. Some engines have a kill switch or button. It may be red and it may be at the end of the throttle handle.

Secure the outboard by turning off and/or disconnecting the fuel supply according to manufacturer's recommendations.

Outboard engines, especially in salt water, should be tilted up and stored with the lower unit out of the water.

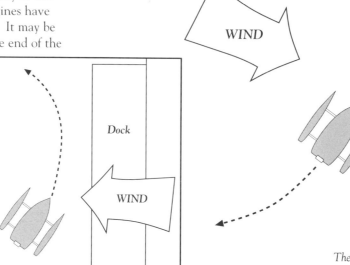

The only way to save yourself from a hard landing when a gust of wind interrupts the approach above is to get some sternway, back out and try again. Wind blowing you away from the dock (left) creates only embarrassment at having to come around again.

Assistance on the dock always helps.

Safety first (and last). Remove the fuel supply to keep the gas in the tank where it belongs.

CHAPTER 3

UNDER SAIL

SAILING KNOWLEDGE

"There seems indeed a remarkable conformity between these islands and those of the opposite hemisphere, not only in their situation, but in their number, and in the manners, customs, arts and manufactures of the inhabitants, tho' it can scarce be imagined that they could ever have any communication, as the globe is now constituted, being at more than 2000 miles distant one from the other, with very little dry land between."

The Journal of Captain Cook's Last Voyage to the Pacific Ocean
–John Rickman

SHALLOW DRAFT SAILING

A boat's draft is the depth from its waterline to the bottom of the keel. Trailerable multihulls are referred to as shoal draft, not because they withstand impact with a shoal any better than other boats, but because they have the ability to navigate in shallower water without running aground. As a result, shoal or shallow draft boats can go lots of places deeper draft boats cannot.

Draft on most deep draft boats comes from a combination of hull and keel protruding below the surface. Modern, fin keel sailboats use a long keel to make up most of that measurement. Deep keels tend to be thinner and have more underwater lift (see Chapter 2) than boats with shallower draft and smaller keels. Higher–aspect ratio keels create more lift with less drag. They perform better allowing the

boat to point higher while close hauled.

So despite the shoal draft boat's ability to sail in shallower waters, you can expect a sacrifice in the boat's ability to sail close to the wind. These boats lack the underwater lift created by a deep keel. Hulls and amas form long, yet shallow keels with low aspect ratio underwa-

Even with a center-board down the modern trailerable multihull sails in shallower water than a comparably sized monohull.

ter lift design. Like stubby sails, stubby keels create less lift.

Most trailerable multi-hulls have the best of both worlds. They use either daggerboard(s) or centerboard(s). With the boards up they may only draw inches. Yet, with the boards down they can sail upwind very efficiently and very close to the wind. And a huge

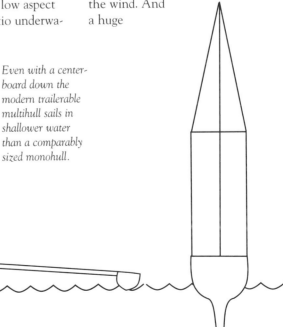

advantage is that boards are normally very high–aspect ratio underwater lift devices with little drag. Expect board boats to sail very well to weather.

A daggerboard is raised and lowered straight up and down while a centerboard swings on an axis. A centerboard's bottom section is raised aft and up into a slot. The daggerboard is a more efficient foil and has less underwater hull drag since it fills the opening into which it retracts.

Centerboards will fold up inside their slots if the boat hits something while underway, which is a tremendous advantage. A daggerboard, on the other hand, would have nowhere to go if it was forced aft and such an impact would probably cause damage to the board and the hull.

Daggerboards and centerboards retract into molded sleeves called trunks. Trimarans generally have one trunk in the main hull and catamarans have one in each hull. Boat builders build tables and other furnishing around centerboard or daggerboard trunks inside cabins to minimize their intrusion.

Another advantage of using boards was illustrated in your Chapter 2 Sailing Skills exercises. Shoal draft multis turn in much tighter circles using their boards.

The beautiful part about board–type boats is that they can sail so well to weather with their boards down. Then, when you decide to head downwind you can pull them up and reduce drag. Boats with fixed keels cannot do that – the drag is there forever.

You may choose to leave the board(s) down or partially down while downwind sailing on a multihull board–boat, particularly with a spinnaker. A course of 45° either side of dead downwind will prove fast and efficient.

You see, the board is pretty heavily loaded with lateral pressure at almost any angle other than dead downwind. This lateral pressure creates lift around the curved surface of the board and actually squirts the boat forward. In other words, if you took a slippery bar of soap, squeezed it with your right hand (the wind's force) against your left hand (the board or lateral resistance), the bar of soap would squirt forward. That's

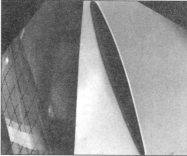

This monohull (top) has plenty of keel area with which to resist leeway.
The daggerboard on this trimaran (middle left) can be easily retracted by one person.
This slot (middle right) fits snugly around the daggerboard optimizing hydrodynamic efficiency under the hull. A partially retracted daggerboard (bottom) adds speed off the wind.

what happens with your board down.

PROS AND CONS OF DEEP DRAFT, SHOAL DRAFT AND BOARDS

DEEP DRAFT PROS
- sails more efficiently and closer to windward
- offers protection to the hulls and rudders from grounding damage (the keel hits first)
- no handling required
- no loss of space in the cabin

DEEP DRAFT CONS
- restricted to deep water
- cannot be launched from a ramp
- cannot beach
- cannot reach shallow gunkholes
- cannot get into some harbors at low tide
- added wetted surface (drag)
- added weight

SHOAL DRAFT (WITHOUT BOARDS) PROS
- hulls and rudders less likely to get damaged from running aground
- no handling of boards required
- not as restricted to water depth
- some can be launched from a ramp
- can get closer to beaches
- can get to shallow gunkholes
- trunks do not take up space in the cabin

SHOAL DRAFT (WITHOUT BOARDS) CONS
- poor performance while beating
- wider turning radius

BOARD BOAT PROS
- not restricted to water depth
- sails more efficiently and closer upwind
- can be launched from a ramp
- can beach
- can reach shallow gunkholes
- can get into more harbors at

low tide
- little added drag
- no added weight

BOARD BOAT CONS
- handling required
- daggerboard offers no protection to the hulls and rudders from grounding damage
- takes up space in the cabin

Shallow draft, cruising sailboats enjoy the option of visiting far more ports than their deep

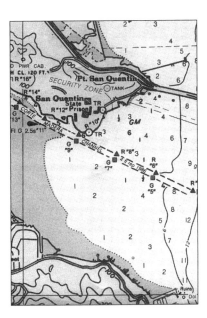

Multihull sailors often say, "channel, what channel?" There are far fewer places where they have to watch their depth.

draft friends. For example, if you were planning a trip down the Florida east coast in a boat that draws around 6 feet, you could safely navigate in only 6 harbors. In a multihull with boards, there are 16 harbors that could accommodate you. This offers a great deal more peace of mind, knowing there are more places of refuge you can get into if trouble strikes.

EFFECTS OF WINDAGE

We call the amount of hull and rigging surface a boat presents to the wind, windage. Given enough wind, most sailboats can sail under bare poles. Sometimes they just blow downwind but sailboats can make forward way from their own windage.

Most trailerable multihulls are pretty low and sleek and each hull would have less windage than a comparably sized monohull. However, more than one hull means more total hull area above the waterline. The windward hull may blanket the other hull(s) somewhat when the wind blows directly on the beam. Otherwise, wind can collect on cross beams, tramps and every other part of the boat and its hardware. It would be impossible to generalize about windage on multihulls compared to monohulls. You could almost calculate windage by taking a photograph of the boat from where the wind is blowing. Cut out the solid parts of the boat and you have your windage.

Additionally, turbulent air that contacted one part of the boat may have an effect on other downwind boat parts. Collapsing dodgers and stowing movable gear such as dinghies will help reduce windage.

Leeway, the tendency of a boat to be set to leeward, occurs as a boat moves along at nearly any point of sail other than dead downwind. The amount of windage will affect leeway. Leeway becomes less noticeable as a boat begins to move through the water.

When a boat moves faster over a given distance it experiences less leeway. If a boat takes 20 minutes to travel one mile it will get pushed much further off course than if it takes only 10 minutes to travel the same mile. Assuming

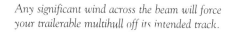
Any significant wind across the beam will force your trailerable multihull off its intended track.

Despite the effects of lift, sails contribute to leeway in a big way.

the wind direction and strength are constant, your 10 minute mile had the wind pushing you to leeward only half as long as your 20 minute mile. You can expect about half as much leeway. Windage will cause leeway under sail as well as under power.

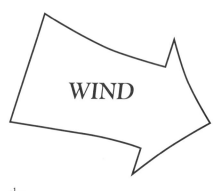
WIND

SEE APPENDIX A FOR SAILING
KNOWLEDGE QUIZ

SAILING SKILLS

SAILING CLOSE HAULED

In order to sail a close–hauled course the board(s) must be down and the sails trimmed in tight. It is very difficult to overtrim a multihull's mainsail. Most people err in the opposite direction and undersheet the main.

If you were to choose errors in your sail trim, you would oversheet the main and undersheet the jib. That way you would be less likely to backwind the main, your big sailing engine.

Backwinding the mainsail is the easiest way to make a boat go slower than it should, yet it is the most difficult to detect. Since there are no magic devices that tell you the main is backwinded, trimming the main harder than

the jib can minimize the probability.

The headsail should also be trimmed in, but not as tightly as the mainsail. Perhaps the closest things you have to a magic backwind detector are telltales, individual strands of colored yarn or magnetic tape attached to the sail.

On the main, a set of telltales should be located about 1/3 the way up and 9" aft of the luff on a rotating mast and about 2' to 3' aft of the luff on a fixed mast. Another set should be located just above the hounds (where the shrouds and forestay connect) and the same location aft of the luff.

Always put the port side telltales a few inches lower than the starboard side. Most of the time you can see the shadow of the telltale behind the sail or it will be visible through a window in the sail. The sun can hit the sails in a

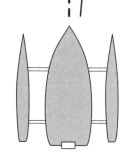

number of ways that make color–coded telltales all turn black. When that happens you cannot tell if you are reading the windward or leeward telltales. So, by always putting the port side lower, you always know which telltale is acting up.

As for the jib, telltale sets should be placed 1/3 and 2/3 of the way up and 9" aft of the luff.

Now let's read the telltales. If your main is sheeted in very tightly, you would see the windward telltale dancing or fluttering around lightly while the backside should be flowing straight back. If the headsail is sheeted properly, the windward telltales would be dancing lightly about the same as the mainsail telltales and the leeward side would be flowing straight back. Fine–tune your main and genoa trim using the control devices discussed in Chapter 2.

Notice that the leeward telltales should always be flowing straight back. Telltales indicate wind flow. We all should know by now that we want the wind to accelerate across the leeward side of the sail, thus causing lift and, in turn, making the sailboat sail. If the telltales dance around, they are telling you the wind is no longer flowing across the backside of the sail and the sail is stalled. If it stalls it is no longer working. If the wing stalls in an airplane the airplane crashes. Ouch! Our sails are nothing more than vertical airplane wings. So keep the backside telltales flowing and your wing won't stall.

Now you are in trim – all the telltales should be reading the same. If one windward telltale is dancing, all telltales will probably join the dance. If one telltale on the backside begins to dance, they should all dance. So, if that is the

case, just pick out the easiest telltale to read and sail by it – after all, it tells you what the entire sail plan is doing.

If the leeward side telltale shows any sign of acting up while sailing to windward, head closer to the wind. If the windward side dances more than usual, you want to turn away from the wind. Since

You're better off living with an oversheeted main and an undersheeted jib than vice versa.

we usually want the windward side telltales to dance a little anyway, it may be a little difficult to read them. But, you will also feel a sharp decline in speed if you are sailing too close to the wind. You know you are sailing way too close to the wind when the leading edge of the headsail starts to curl inward, away from the rest of the sail – bear off when this happens.

To get used to sailing by the telltales, just remember to push the tiller in the direction of the troubled telltale, either windward or leeward. Assuming you are sitting on the windward side and the backside telltale acts up, you push the tiller to leeward. This heads the boat closer to the wind – the telltale will stop acting up and flow aft again. If the windward telltale acts up, pull the tiller toward the windward side and the boat will turn off the wind more and that telltale will flow aft once again. Keep doing this until the movements are small and sure.

A CLOSE REACH

From a close–hauled heading the helmsman needs to bear off about 10 to 20 degrees

Telltales on the sails will provide little or no information while broad reaching and running.

Windward telltale dancing while leeward telltale flows straight back.

All three telltales flow back (left) telling the helmsperson the sail is well trimmed. Slightly out of trim, (right) the telltales all go in different directions but with a tendency toward flowing aft.

that apparent wind is caused by the boat's motion through the water. If you motor 5 knots in dead calm you feel 5 knots of breeze coming directly off the bow. Add some real wind and the direction and speed felt on deck become a combination of the actual or true wind and the wind the boat makes by moving, apparent wind.

By moving faster than a monohull a multihull experiences more apparent wind, just like an iceboat. As an iceboat begins to bear off and head downwind, the speed and resulting apparent wind increase so dramatically the boat is actually sailing downwind with the sail set as if going to weather. And, like multihulls, this ability is caused by less resistant drag – the ice boat has very little drag as its blades just skim across the ice.

BEAM REACH

Once again the helmsman does the same gradual bearing off and now instructs the crew to ease the sheets of the mainsail and the headsail slightly. The key is to watch the leeward telltale – it must keep flowing aft. If it doesn't, ease the sheet.

With the wind nearly on the beam you present the areas of highest windage directly to the wind. You can expect maximum leeway on or around this point of sail. Don't be lulled into thinking it's time to pull your board(s) up just because the wind you feel on your face has abated. You'll still need to resist that leeway.

BROAD REACH AND RUNNING

The helmsman again bears off and the sheets are also eased the same way they were going from a close reach to a beam reach. At this point, all that great reaching speed will begin to

onto a close reach. If the helmsman turns slowly the sails may not have to be eased at all. As the boat slowly bears off it will pick up more speed. You can expect about the same trim you had going to

weather. The key here is to watch the backside telltales. The second you see them begin not flowing aft, you need to ease the sheet until they do.

Beginning sailors learn

diminish somewhat. The sails should be eased, keeping the backside telltales flowing. On boats with fixed masts, however, forget the idea of getting the backside telltales on the mainsail to flow. The fixed mast will cause the wind to stall most of the way back along the sail.

Multihulls usually sail downwind on a broad reach. They seldom sail much deeper than 45° either side of dead downwind. Slower, poorer performing boats will probably do better by sailing a little deeper, but any of the higher performance boats will get to a downwind destination much earlier by "tacking" downwind.   In other words, sailing at 45° angles either side of dead downwind and jibing through 90° just the opposite of sailing to weather.

JIBING

Most monohull sailors are taught to do a controlled jibe. The main is sheeted in, the helm put over and the mainsheet is eased quickly as the wind changes sides of the sail. These precautions are taken to reduce any risk of the boom swinging violently across the cockpit and damaging the rigging or, more important, a person.

The boom tends to swing violently because the typical monohull is limited in speed. Let's say the wind is blowing 15 knots, while the boat is going 5 knots. When you jibe, the boom can swing across under the power of a 10 knot breeze. This can make for a lot of stress on the rigging.

On faster multihulls, however, this is not necessarily so. A jibe can certainly be done that way, if you wish. But keep in mind, multihulls sail downwind at speeds nearly equal to that of the wind. In 15 knots of wind the multihull may be going 13 knots, making a difference of only 2 knots. That

Communication and teamwork go a long way to keep the boat sailing smooth and fast.

would not make for a violent jibe.

The most important part of the jibe is to alert the crew with the warning, "ready to jibe." Do not jibe until the crew is tending the sheets and sails and reply, "Ready."

When jibing from a broad reach be sure not to head down

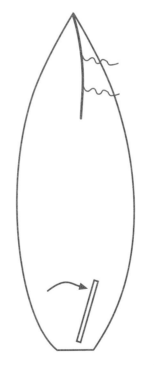

Pushing the tiller toward the distressed telltale (in this case the leeward tale) will get the boat back into trim.

deep before you actually jibe – this slows the boat way down to monohull speeds and a violent jibe may occur after all. Instead, make the turn with steadily increasing pressure on the helm, and then after steering about 90° or more through the turn, straighten the helm and again sail by the telltales on a broad reach.

You may need to use other means such as landmarks or the compass to find your 45° position on either side of the downwind track. Sailing upwind you have the advantage of luffing sails until you turn about 45° off the wind. With the wind over the stern don't expect any luffing except, perhaps, when the jib is blanketed by the mainsail.

BACK TO CLOSE HAULED

From a broad reach the helmsman alerts the crew to trim the sails. Then the boat heads up. The crew should be sure to avoid overtrimming the sails and causing the leeward telltales to act up. They need to flow aft at all times.

Follow the same procedure for each step of reaching until the sails are again tightly trimmed for going to weather and the helmsman needs only to steer by that favorite telltale.

TACKING

In order to tack a multi-hull efficiently you must be sailing close to the wind with the board(s) down and the mainsail sheeted in tightly. Trying to tack from a reach often causes confusion for skipper and crew. Turning from an angle greater than 45° off the wind makes it harder to tell when the boat goes into irons, especially if the sails were trimmed correctly for the reach. A wider arc and imprecise entry into irons makes it more difficult to find the close hauled course on the new tack.

The helmsman must alert the crew with the warning, "ready about," and be sure the crew is manning the working sheet, the lazy sheet and the mainsheet. The helmsman always waits to hear the crew reply "Ready" before initiating the tack.

To tack, the helm goes over with steadily increasing pressure, and comes back to the center line just before the boat hits the 45° position on the new tack. If the rudder is slammed over it will act more like a brake, slowing the boat rather than turning it and carrying momentum through the turn. If the helm turns too gently and doesn't turn far enough, the boat will sail up into the wind, lose speed, and its momentum probably won't take it through the tack.

Remember that extra weight and bulk that restricts a monohull's speed also makes it harder to stop once it starts moving. It's the same momentum principle that affects a big truck going down a hill. A monohull will tend to keep moving much further after the sails are de–powered.

The mainsheet should be tight when the tack is initiated and eased when the bow goes through the wind. It will help turn the boat by acting like the flat end of a weathervane. The bigger, flatter end of the weathervane presents more wind resistance and gets blown downwind. The smaller, pointy end goes up into the wind. That same effect causes the back part of the boat, where the mainsail is presenting a flat surface to the wind, to blow downwind.

After the boat goes through the wind, however, you no longer want the weathervane effect so you must ease the mainsheet a foot or two. By easing the sheet you will accomplish two things. First, it takes the pressure off the leech of the main, taking

Sailing with the wind across the beam is best done with the board(s) down.

away the weathervane effect. Second, it will make the sail a little fuller and, therefore, more powerful when it fills on the new side. It acts sort of like shifting down to second gear when rounding a tight curve in your car.

The headsail sheet should be completely released from the winch just as the sail begins to luff. The lazy sheet trimmer should take up all the slack in the sheet prior to the tack and, after taking no more than two wraps on the winch, begin trimming as the headsail fills on the new tack.

Most trimarans tend to tack as fast as monohulls. Consequently, the helmsman wants to slow the rate of the turn just as the headsail crosses the bow. The trimmer can then sheet in the headsail hand over hand while the sail and sheet are slack. With that head start on trimming, the crew has less of a chore making the final sail trim.

Wind in the sheeted sail will help push the bow to leeward and aid in completing the turn. If the turn is not slowed after going through the wind, the headsail could blow further off to leeward. When it fills, added pressure on the sheet means a lot of grinding to get the proper trim. The crew tends to get tired and angry when this happens a few times. Watch out for mutinous behavior.

Many catamarans and some trimarans don't tack as quickly as monohulls. Long waterlines are to blame. In this case more boat means more drag so having more than one hull is similar to having one long hull.

Designers of some trailerable multihulls have managed to minimize this effect so it will vary from one boat to the next.

A slow tacking boat should keep its jib cleated when it goes into irons. The sheet can be eased out slightly creating a rounded pocket in the sail. As the bows pass through the wind the jib backwinds and helps push the bow around. When the bows are about 45° beyond the wind source, release the jib. Extra grinding is all but guaranteed so keep an eye on the crew's mood.

Trailerable multihull sailors that sail in heavy seas and

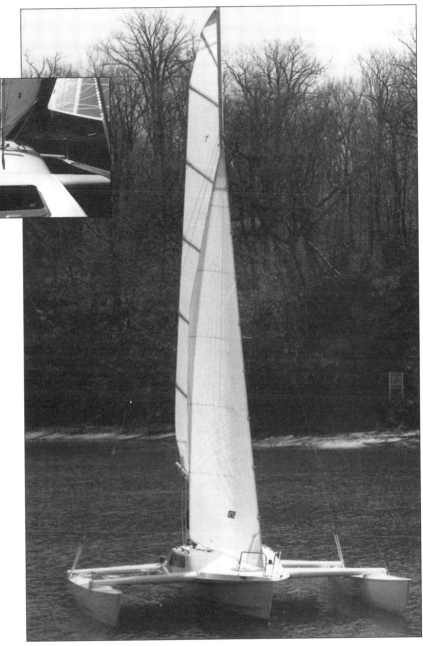

Sailing upwind, close hauled, a tack is simply a matter of putting the tiller over, releasing the jib sheet and trimming the opposite jib sheet. Onboard before a jibe, (inset) everyone pays particular attention not to jibe accidentally.

winds may have no choice but to backwind their headsail during tacks. Added windage and wave action may drastically slow the boat while the sails luff and forward thrust is suspended.

SAILING DRILLS

To practice all these maneuvers you should set out two marks that form a perpendicular line with the wind source (a perfect beam reach from one to the other). Start with the buoys pretty far apart allowing plenty of room for the drill. As you and your crew get better and more efficient, close the gap between marks.

There are four ways you can use these marks to help improve your multihull sailing skills.

Drill #1 Sail around the marks leaving them both to port.

Begin this exercise by approaching the right mark. Trim and head up to close hauled. Tack after you have sailed clear of the mark. Bear off to a reach and ease sheets. As you reach the left mark, bear off to a broad reach and ease sheets. Immediately after passing the mark warn the crew and jibe. Gain control of the boat on a broad reach on the new tack, then go back up to a beam reach. Repeat the exercise until your team can make it look smooth and easy. Then move everyone to a new position and start again.

Drill #2 Sail around the marks leaving them both to starboard.

Here's a great way to test the crew. Anyone can learn to perform the same task over and over if he/she is given proper instructions. With everything reversed, the crew and skipper really need to know their stuff to achieve the same fluid motion you got with the port roundings.

Drill #3 Figure 8 tacking

Tack the way you did leaving the right mark to port. After the tack, bear off to a beam reach and then a broad reach. Set your course for a spot about a boat length to leeward of the left mark. Approach the mark for a starboard rounding. When you are abeam and to leeward of the mark, begin heading up and trimming sheets until close hauled and then tack. Immediately bear off to a reach, broad reach, and when approaching the right mark for a port rounding, head up and trim for close hauled and tack again. Keep this up. It's great tacking and trimming practice.

Drill #4 Figure 8 jibing

By this time you should be able to guess the rules. Start from a close hauled course anywhere between the two marks. Once you are to windward of the imaginary line that runs between the marks, reach toward the one that you don't have to tack to get to. Round it by jibing then immediately head up and set a course about one boat length to windward of the other mark. When you pass it jibe again and repeat the exercise until you and your crew are ready for the America's Cup.

Backwinding the jib may help tack the boat when it has very little way on or if waves prevent it from turning upwind.

Easing the mainsheet after a tack will help prevent unintentionally re-tacking.

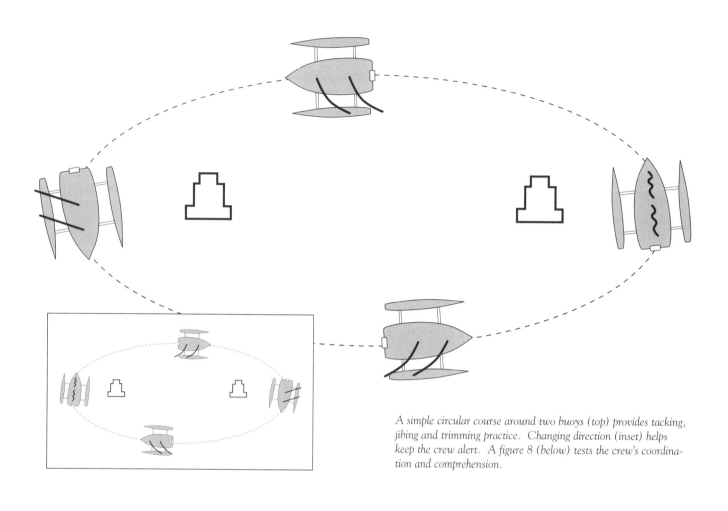

A simple circular course around two buoys (top) provides tacking, jibing and trimming practice. Changing direction (inset) helps keep the crew alert. A figure 8 (below) tests the crew's coordination and comprehension.

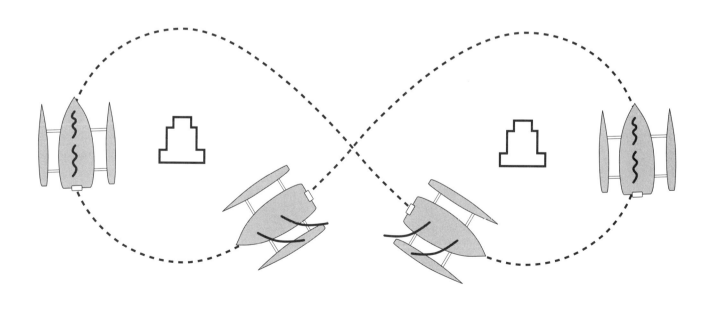

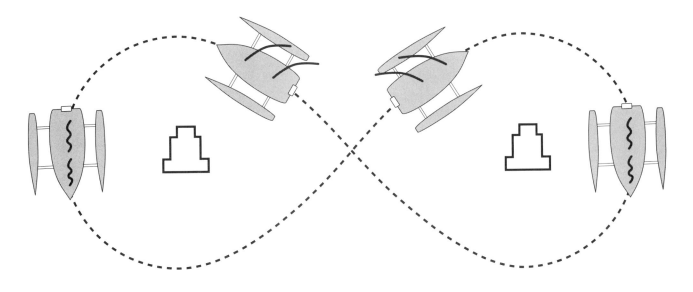

With a little concentration, changing direction can be accomplished without interrupting the crew's flow. Remember to concentrate on the boat in relation to the wind direction. If you can keep your eye on the fundamentals, everything else will fall into place.

STAYING ON A COMPASS COURSE

The best way to learn steering a compass course is to NOT use the compass. Most people radically oversteer in the early stages of compass use because the compass does not react immediately. It takes a little time for the compass to actually read correctly. So the natural instinct is to keep turning until something happens. By the time it does, you're heading way beyond your intended course. The only way to fix it is to steer back in the other direction where the same thing happens. Pretty soon you're going around in circles.

To learn how to steer by compass, pick something on the horizon at some angle close to the bow and steer for it. That something may be a mark, a buoy, a cer-

tain cloud, a star, or whatever. By now you should be used to steering toward an object.

Now, refer to the compass. What is the heading? Just for the sake of discussion, let's say you're on 270°.

Next, looking out at the environment, turn the boat a little bit to one side or the other. Find something new to steer toward. Straighten out and maintain a new course. Check your compass. Still on 270? Probably not. Note the new compass course. Then correct your heading on the original object.

Look back at the compass. Try to get back to your previous course looking only at the compass. Keep doing this and then begin looking more at the compass than at your object.

A nice little learning trick is to pretend the compass lubber line is the bow of the boat. If your object or 270° on the compass is to the left, turn left. The same goes when the lubber line is on the the other side of your intended course.

Keeping in mind that the compass doesn't react immediately, you must make a small correction and then wait about a half minute for the compass to settle down. Then take a reading. The compass usually doesn't noticeably move every time the bow moves back and forth. Make small to moderate corrections then wait to see the result in the compass heading. Watch the bow to see how much it turns compared to the compass. As in all things related to sailing, practice makes perfect.

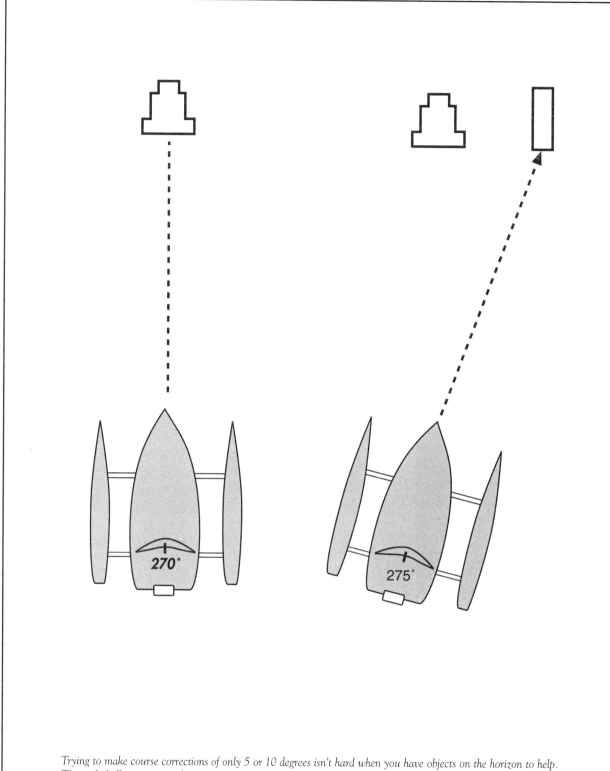

Trying to make course corrections of only 5 or 10 degrees isn't hard when you have objects on the horizon to help. The real challenge comes when it's just you and the compass.

CHAPTER 4

CRUISING

SAILING KNOWLEDGE

"At this moment I don't understand. The boat mounts a wave, heels incredibly, and instead of going over the crest, continues mounting. The starboard float gets caught, the water boils. Denis and I exchange a look of disbelief: "We can't be going over!"

Capsize
-Nicholas Angel

Fit your harness to your body on dry land if possible. Like most other things, it's more difficult underway. You also may want to adjust it to fit over your outerwear if it is likely you will have a jacket or foul weather gear on under your harness.

Sailboats underway, regardless of size, style, or the body of water on which they sail, bring us into an environment that can pose threats to our well-being. Tradition dictates skippers assume responsibility for the crew and ship. However, sailors must learn their own safety procedures to care for themselves as well as to assist the skipper when necessary.

In addition to a personal flotation device, each sailor should have a safety harness and it should be worn after dark or during bad weather. Safety harnesses should also be worn by people on deck when seas are moderate to heavy and winds pick up. Your basic, on-deck strategy should come from the familiar saying, "One hand for you and one hand for the boat." Your harness will ensure you stay with the boat if holding on isn't enough.

Harnesses fit securely around the upper body and have a tether line that attaches to the boat. A good harness is usually made of webbing material with strong stainless steel fittings such as "D" rings onto which the tether snaps. A modern version of the safety harness combines an inflatable personal flotation device (PFD) with the harness. Some of these hybrid PFDs have recently been approved by the U.S. Coast Guard.

Sailors using these PFDs get the best of two worlds — one, a safety harness to keep you with the boat, and two, if you do go overboard, the inflatable PFD has more flotation than many conventional PFDs. Some of the more expensive foul weather gear jackets have built in harnesses as well. All this gear can be found at any good marine store.

Some folks think that all they have to do is put on a safety harness and they'll be safe regardless of where they attach to the boat. This is not so! Some points of attachment are not stable.

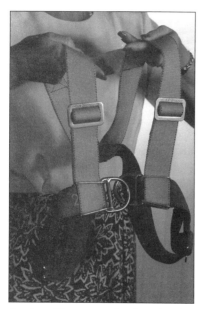

Sturdy webbing material and reinforced seams are essential elements of a well-constructed harness.

An example of the recently approved personal inflatable PFDs.

For example, NEVER hook up to a lifeline. The word "lifeline" is a misnomer. It's easy to push it beyond its limit and have it become a "deathline."

So find sturdy attachment points on the boat, such as shrouds, or maybe a through-bolted cleat or padeye. CAUTION! Take care not to snap into a screwed-in cleat or padeye. With nothing more than a threaded screw or bolt to keep it attached, you may end up in the water with a piece of hardware dangling from the end of your tether. You may only be able to determine which deck hardware is through-bolted by looking on the back or inside of hulls, decks, amas, etc. It's worth the time and effort.

The absolute best way to hook up to the boat is to run strong lines from forward cleats to aft cleats on both sides of the mast. They're called "jacklines." Boats that undertake serious offshore passages often make jacklines from plastic coated cable,

similar to lifelines.

Crew members attach, the quick-release clip at the end of their tether to the jackline and they have safe access to the entire boat. First time multihull sailors should check the length of their tethers. Beamier boats mean greater distances from the outer hull or ama to the mast and deck areas. Insufficient tether length could leave you barking at the end of a short leash.

Without jacklines crew members must unhook and rehook as they move about the boat. Time spent unhooked is time when a sailor could get washed overboard. Don't take that chance — use jacklines.

Capsizing

Unfortunately, many people unfamiliar with multihulls feel compelled to ask questions like, "...they do go over, right?" What a scary thought. Where do you suppose that idea came from? Of course, from watching those little

beach cats zip around in the surf or on the bay. And sure, once in a while a gust hits and over they go sending bathing–suited sailors for a refreshing dip. In most cases these little skitterers are back up and running in a few minutes.

Keep in mind the power to weight ratio of a beach cat is extremely high. There's a lot of sail area and very little weight which is why they capsize so easily.

It's a different deal with cruising multihulls. The power to weight ratio is much lower. For example, the Elan 7.7 Swing Wing Trimaran carries only 310 feet of sail on a boat that weighs 1300 pounds and is over 19' wide.

Compare that with beach cats that often carry as much as 400 feet of sail area on a 400 pound boat that is only 8 feet 6 inches wide. They may add 400 more feet of sail area when the spinnaker goes up. You can see that 310 square feet of sail for a 1300 pound boat is a lot different than 800 feet of sail for a 400 pound boat.

The same kind of relationship exists between cartop dinghies, such as Sunfish and Lasers, and monohull keelboats. So why don't you hear, "...they do go over, right," when people set eyes on their first keelboat? Just like the question about whether the refrigerator light stays on when the door is closed, we may never know.

Most multihulls will not capsize even under intense conditions. But, what if the unlikely capsize should occur? Then what? Follow the advice sailors have heeded for years, "Stay with the boat!"

One argument multihull fanatics give for their obsession is that multihulls do not sink. Why? Because, if you remember, they use their breadth to stay upright — they don't use ballasted keels to keep the deck pointing skyward. Without that extra weight they float, and they float very well.

Additionally, almost all multihulls have flotation built in. With all that flotation and some trapped air, multihulls are literally unsinkable, just like Molly!

Ballasted monohulls in the same condition sink like a stone, leaving you stuck in a dangerous rubber raft, if you're lucky enough to have one.

The multihull is a raft, a very large, safe one. One catamaran was run down by a ship in the Gulf Stream off Miami — it turned up in England months later, still floating. Sure, it was upside down, but it was floating.

A catamaran boat designer was overheard at a boat show saying, "Well, the only thing a keel will do is guarantee you'll be right-side-up when the boat hits bottom." As a multihull sailor you can expect hours of lively discourse with monohull devotees who think you're nuts. It's best to prepare your arguments in advance.

(Above) Beach cats can and do get their sailors wet. Chances are remote the same thing will happen with the trailerable tri. (Below)

PREVENTION: THE BEST CURE

Most multihulls, once capsized, will require outside help to get them tipped back upright.

It's still extremely unlikely you'll ever have to deal with a capsize. We minimize that possibility by prudent sailing and decision making. Multihulls, by their very nature, may not help you in your quest for prudence. They aren't good at telling you they have problems until the problems are severe.

Suppose you are sailing along on a monohull keelboat and the wind picks up. The boat heels and doesn't go any faster. You put a reef in the sail to reduce heeling and the problem disappears. When the wind picks up even more, you heel and lose speed. Solve this problem with another reef or smaller headsail.

In multihulls, when the wind picks up the boat goes faster but signs of overpowering are much more subtle. The skipper on a multihull must learn to recognize minor changes in his or her boat and make proper adjustments.

Judgment comes with experience and it is impossible to generalize about a class of boats (trailerable multihulls) with so many variations. However, what follows are some hints you may find helpful in reading the wind and sea conditions. They should help you take the precautions necessary to maintain safety. Boats with knotmeters will have an easier time reading wind strength but all multihull sailors should be able to recognize the physical changes that occur to the boat when the wind increases.

15 KNOTS

With a full main and genoa, watch for the leeward hull/ama to get washed over occasionally. You may also feel some resistance in the helm. Overall, you will just feel exhilarated and want more. It's O.K. You can handle it.

20 KNOTS

Watch for the leeward hull/ama to be awash more consistently. A rooster tail may develop at the bow. The helm may have slightly more weight and it could "ventilate," losing control momentarily.

Take a reef and seriously consider shifting to a working jib.

Depending on your point of sail your boat speed could be well above 15 knots. If a dangerous situation arises it will arise quickly. Keep your hand on the mainsheet, ready to spill the breeze at a second's notice.

25 KNOTS

Things haven't changed drastically from 20 knots except the working jib is no longer an option, it is a necessity.

30 KNOTS

The leeward hull/ama is depressed further. The boat may tend to plane and the helmsman should pay close attention to how the bows move through approaching waves. If you sail into waves, as opposed to over them, pitchpoling (flipping over bow first) is a possibility. Speed needs to be reduced to avoid this. Take a second reef.

30+ KNOTS

Sea conditions associated with winds of this strength create a perfect environment for capsizing and pitchpoling. Set a storm jib or go bare headed with a third reef if your sail has one.

When the windward hull or ama flies high out of the water, you know you have way too much sail area up. When the leeward hull or ama wants to dig its bow deep in the water, again you are over canvassed. Reef early and sacrifice a little of that speed for the sake of safety.

HEAVY WEATHER SAILING

You should know the boat you are sailing and its capabilities. There are some larger multihulls that simply are not designed for anything but coastal and inland cruising. All boats, including multihulls, fall into classifications

A little more heeling and this monohull will need to reef its mainsail.

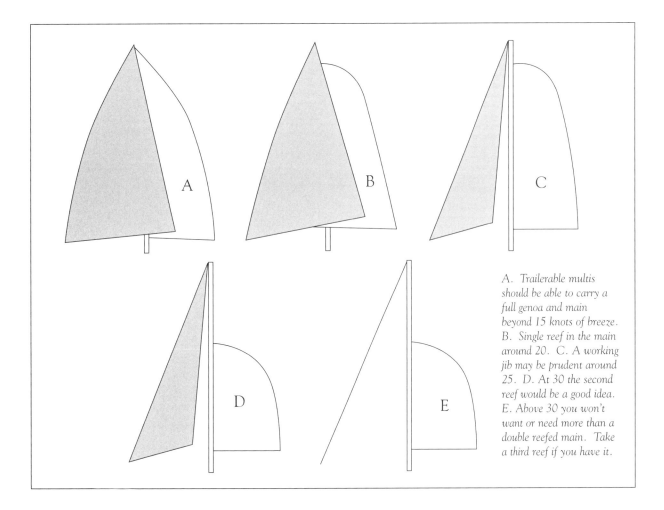

A. Trailerable multis should be able to carry a full genoa and main beyond 15 knots of breeze. B. Single reef in the main around 20. C. A working jib may be prudent around 25. D. At 30 the second reef would be a good idea. E. Above 30 you won't want or need more than a double reefed main. Take a third reef if you have it.

based on their intended use. You should not be caught hundreds of miles from safe harbor in a boat that was designed only for daysailing. Always check the weather before setting out on a trip, and be sure you and your boat are prepared for whatever weather is forecast.

On the other hand, there are some extremely well–built multihulls that can withstand severe ocean conditions with no problems whatsoever. Multihulls really come into their own when you consider the speed/time factor. Traveling at a consistently faster clip means shorter travel times. And less time at sea reduces your chance of getting hit by a surprise storm or front.

Comfort also plays a role in multihull cruising. Long coastal passages on a monohull that is laid over on its side, pounding and wallowing, can leave sailors pretty exhausted. The same passage on a

The sinking bow and associated bow wake on this leeward ama let you know it's got a load on it.

In light winds this trailerable will sail as flat as an aircraft carrier.

Downwind sailing can be flat and safe until the wind and swell kicks up.

You should know basic, adverse weather safety routines by now. This list combines basic storm precautions with some additional considerations for multihull sailors.

- Run jacklines
- Deploy safety harnesses, PFDs and foul weather gear
- Shorten sails
- Secure all hatches, ports and windows
- Pump bilges dry and keep checking for water in the hulls
- Secure all loose gear
- Locate and clear access to emergency safety gear such as pumps, bailers and sea anchor
- Get a good position fix and update your position on the chart
- Make plans for altering your course to sheltered waters or safe harbor

TACTICS

Multihulls go very fast in heavy winds, even with shortened sails. While sailing to windward you will probably begin to encounter large seas. Depending on the distance between waves, you may have to alter your sailing technique. If the seas are very steep and close you may want to ease off the sails to slow the boat down. Otherwise you will find yourself banging hard into each of these short, steep waves.

If the seas are large, yet the wave crests are far enough apart, you can sail very smoothly while close hauled. You want to steer in pinch mode (close hauled tending to go slightly into irons) up the face of the wave and bear away down the backside of the wave. Avoid sailing so close to the wind that you go into irons or accidentally tack while the crew is not prepared. The combination of

comparable size multihull can be a pleasure. For one thing, you will always sail flat. Most people prefer "horizontal" to the various alternatives.

Since you are sailing more comfortably, you will not tire as easily from simple tasks such as walking around the boat. Most sailors dread using the head on a healing monohull. Simply maintaining your position until you're done can wear you out. Pursuit of

simple, creature comforts on the multihull are heaven by comparison. Remember, a rested crew is a safer and more efficient crew.

Yet another beautiful aspect of the multihull is its safer, wide open, non-heeling deck. Foredeck apes (people who get put to work while others watch) who bring sails down, lash down gear, or secure hatches, appreciate not having to do acrobatics just to keep from falling overboard.

a backwinded headsail and the crest of a huge wave could knock the boat over backward.

Should the wind be heavy enough to lift your windward hull or ama, you need to put on a lot of downhaul, tease the boat closer to the wind to keep the hull or ama down and ease your traveler a little. This spills some wind and flattens the boat.

Downhaul is an important device for flattening the mainsail on fractional rig boats. The flatter the sail the easier it is to sail in heavy winds. The downhaul actually bends the mast, flattening the sail. It also allows the top of the sail to twist off away from the wind, depowering the top of the mainsail. Lowering the power button still gives the boat plenty of power down lower, which equates to plenty of speed and less heeling.

When the winds are really heavy you should not try to sail on a reach of any kind — the combination of heavy gusts and waves could cause a lot of problems. For example, if a huge gust lifted the windward hull and a wave hit at the same time the boat could wind up high up on its side. It wouldn't take much more force to put the boat all the way over.

If you must sail on a reach, reduce sail to bare minimum. In extreme conditions bare poles may even be enough.

Sailing downwind will be very fast. If a large gust should hit while sailing on a broad reach, bear away to keep the boat sailing flat. This reaction is just the opposite of what was recommended while going to weather. When the hull or ama began to fly on a beat, you headed up. Here, if the hull or ama begins to fly, you need to head down away from the wind.

Heading down gives the boat more chance to use all of its flotation. Heading up could cause the boat to heal further and wave action could cause a disaster. Unfortunately, bearing away increases the possibility of accidentally jibing. All helm adjustments in such cases are critical.

HEAVING–TO

When conditions deteriorate beyond your ability to safely sail the boat, heaving-to offers the best means of survival. In short, heaving-to is stopping the boat with the bow about 45° off the wind. Variety in weather conditions, boat design, construction and equipment make it impossible to recommend a means of heaving-to that will work in all cases. The key is to keep the boat from sailing forward on either the sails or spars and hulls.

It is important to recognize at this point that the commonly accepted method of heaving-to on a monohull may not work on a multihull. In other words, simply backing the jib, feathering the mainsail and tying the tiller to leeward may not get the boat to stop.

Your last, and perhaps most reliable, method of heaving-to is to set your sea anchor. Trailerable multis engaged in coastal cruising will rarely find themselves faced with such a drastic means of survival. Monitoring weather forecasts and the relative-

Your trailerable multihull may heave-to by backing the jib and putting the tiller to leeward, but don't count on it.

The differences between monohull and multihull hull shapes makes rafting an achievable challenge.

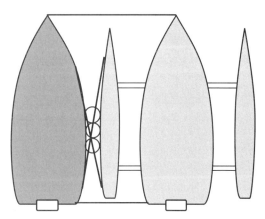

Rafting boats of dissimilar size or type calls for lots of fenders. Line them up in places you know the boats will touch and other places where they could come into contact.

Easy steps for rafting

- Securely anchor or tie the first boat to a dock.
- Park boat 2 alongside a foot or two away.
- Pass lines from one to the other.
- Draw boats together by pulling lines or using boat 2's propeller forces in short bursts.
- Set lots of fenders between the boats.
- Adjust lines so that boats make contact at their beams.
- Stagger spreaders. (Most multi hulls will have their spreaders well inside the amas or hulls so this will not be as critical as it is with monohulls.)

A tight fit is better as long as both boats can rise and fall with the tide. Use one line to attach bows and another to attach sterns. Springlines should attach to a forward point on one boat and an aft point on the other. This

ly short duration of coastal passages on these quick vessels offer a margin of safety offshore sailors don't always enjoy.

Longer trips along routes that stretch further from safe harbors increase the likelihood of having to heave-to for extended periods of time. See Chapter 8 in the Cruising Catamaran section for a detailed description on use of sea anchors and drogues.

rafting a monohull and multihull together could be problematic. As with most sailing problems, proper technique and equipment offer a solution.

Use at least two fenders, a bow and stern line, and two springlines. Fenderboards are also a big help as are extra helping hands.

RAFTING AT ANCHOR

Rafting is simply tying two or more boats together, either at anchor or at a dock. At some time or another, all sailors might find themselves having to raft. The biggest difference you will find between monohulls and multihulls is that most monohulls have very rounded sides, while the multihull's lines are longer and straighter. Rafting anything to a monohull means making contact at only one area and stretching long lines between parts of the boat that don't come close to one another. Because of these differences some folks think

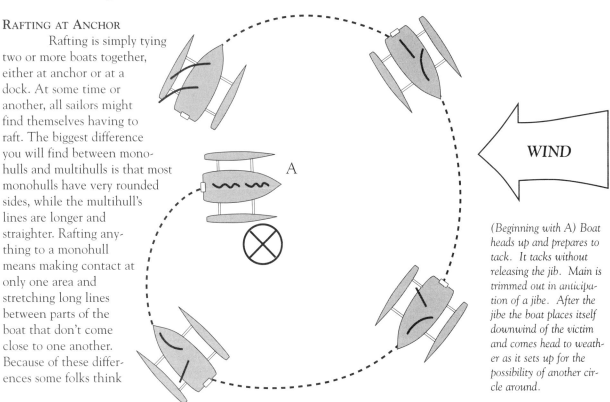

(*Beginning with A*) *Boat heads up and prepares to tack. It tacks without releasing the jib. Main is trimmed out in anticipation of a jibe. After the jibe the boat places itself downwind of the victim and comes head to weather as it sets up for the possibility of another circle around.*

will prevent them from sliding forward and aft and possibly dislodging the fenders.

It doesn't matter whether the boats rafting are monohulls or multihulls — any combination will work. All of the standard techniques, guidelines and etiquette of rafting are the same.

Always have the largest boat in the middle and anchored when rafting at anchor.

CAUTION: Do not raft when bad weather is predicted. Wind and seas can cause a lot of damage to boats when they rub and bump each other. Leaving in a hurry may also become impossible for boats that aren't at the ends of the raft.

SEE APPENDIX A FOR SAILING
KNOWLEDGE QUIZ

SAILING SKILLS

MAN OVERBOARD

The American Sailing Association keelboat certification system devotes more attention to crew overboard recovery than, perhaps, any other single topic. There's a good reason for this disparate concentration on one subject. Occasionally people fall off boats and those who remain onboard need to know how to react.

Mastering overboard return and recovery techniques in 20 to 30 foot Basic Keelboat Sailing boats doesn't automatically qualify you to perform a similar maneuver in a multihull. It may take practice and adjustment of your existing skills as well as mastery of some new skills to get the job done on a new boat.

As you venture into the multihull world it will become apparent these aren't just different size boats, they are entirely different boats. Practicing and becom-

(Clockwise from upper left) 1. Person falls overboard; helmsman heads up. 2. The boat tacks. 3. Bearing away with the victim in sight. 4. After jibing it's time to sail out beyond the victim and come head to wind.

ing comfortable with overboard drills will ensure crew safety and increase your confidence.

THE QUICK STOP

This very popular method of returning to a swimmer requires the boat to turn abruptly as soon as the person enters the water. The vessel then circles the victim until it can execute a slow, controlled approach. In some cases the person in the water may have to be circled more than once.

THE QUICK STOP DRILL

Use a cushion or fender to practice using the following techniques.

1 As soon as the cushion hits the water someone yells "Man Overboard."

2 In an actual overboard situation, a crew member throws a type IV PFD to the victim.

3 Someone, possibly the person who yelled, should then be assigned to point at the victim and keep him or her in sight at all times.

4 Regardless of point of sail, the boat must head up immediately and tack.

On a monohull you simply use the boat's momentum during and after a tack to get to windward and around the victim. Then you bear away. Backwinding the jib helps turn the boat in a tighter circle.

If your trailerable multi was performing true to form, quickness has carried it a few boat lengths away from the cushion in just the time it took to accomplish 2, 3 and 4. Regardless of your point of sail, you will probably find yourself too far away to simply circle the victim by tacking and immediately bearing away. You should be ready to tack and sail to windward of the victim on your new tack.

5 Bear away and prepare to jibe.

If you manage to tack quickly enough, and with enough momentum to pass the victim to windward, you may want to backwind the jib just as you would on a monohull. You will turn and jibe faster.

6 Jibe, continue turning and heading up on your new tack and prepare to come alongside the victim.

In theory, the Quick Stop enables sailors to keep trying until they get it right. By turning around the victim in ever-tightening circles the boat eventually slows and stops where it can do some good. Proponents of the Quick Stop often say all you have to do is push the helm over and eventually you'll get the victim. It may work out that way on some monohulls in some conditions. But don't expect it to be that easy on a multihull.

In practice it takes work to get the boat to behave the way it should. Speed and momentum differences will create different results.

While the Quick Stop's speed and simplicity have won many advocates, proximity to the victim is perhaps the most compelling reason for its popularity. Traveling further away from the victim reduces your chances of reuniting boat and swimmer.

FIGURE 8 RETURN

1 As soon as the cushion hits the water the first person to notice yells "Man Overboard."

2 In an actual overboard situation a crew member throws a type IV PFD to the victim.

3 Someone should then be assigned to point at the victim and keep him or her in sight at all times.

4 Get the boat sailing on a beam reach.

5 Sail away at least 5 but not more than 10 boat lengths.

While sailing away sounds like the wrong thing to do, keep in mind you want to get the victim on the first attempt. This means you need to get organized — the helmsman needs some distance to correctly execute the next steps and the crew needs time to get everything ready.

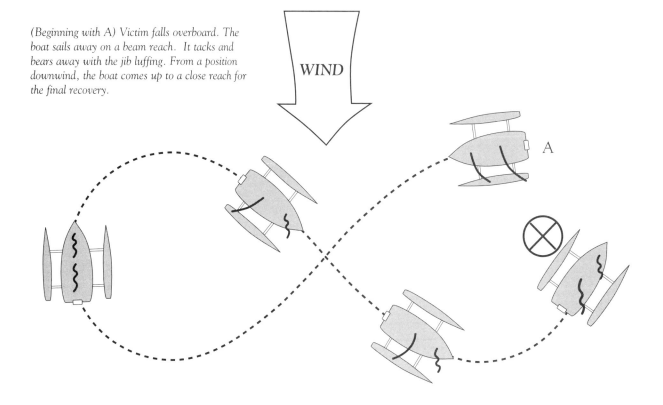

(Beginning with A) Victim falls overboard. The boat sails away on a beam reach. It tacks and bears away with the jib luffing. From a position downwind, the boat comes up to a close reach for the final recovery.

WIND

A

6 Change tacks and sail back on a beam reach.

With a trimaran you can either tack or jibe, but, with the catamaran you must jibe — it is much easier and takes less tending of the sails. Remember our tacking drills? Cats will not tack from a reach. So, jibing creates fewest problems.

After the jibe, just keep letting the jib luff — you don't want much speed now anyway, although you do want to have enough speed to control the boat.

7 Sail toward the victim aiming for a spot about four or five boat lengths downwind.

You want to make the final approach on a close reach. That way you can sheet in to make the boat go forward, should you fall short; or luff the sail if you are approaching with too much speed. Heading to leeward of the victim ensures you can point higher (close reach) on the final approach.

Two sets of hands are better than one when it comes to reefing a fully battened mainsail. One continuous reefing line (above, inset) makes easy work of reefing this sail.

8 Line up 3 to 4 boat lengths away from the victim and get the boat onto a close reach.

9 Luff the sails and stop beside the victim.

Remember the boat must be nearly stopped to adequately help the victim into the boat. If you fall short and are too far to leeward, you will quickly drift away from the victim.

Stop beside the victim and to leeward. Stopping to windward of the person might cause the wind and waves to push the boat down on top of him or her.

You must know your boat and how it performs in various wind and wave conditions to execute these maneuvers correctly. Don't rely on past experiences – practice.

REEFING

Jiffy reefing has become, by far, the most popular method of reducing sail. Reefing lines are kept rigged in grommets along the

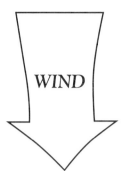

WIND

The easiest way to heave-to is to tack without releasing the jib, luff the main and put the tiller all the way down to leeward.

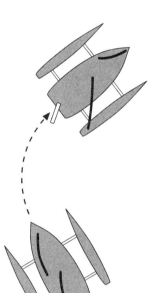

sail area you had up before reefing. Be sure to get that foot tight.

It's as easy as one, two, three.

To start, let's sail the boat as close to the wind as we can with the jib trimmed and the mainsheet loose. Now, be sure the topping lift is attached so the boom won't crash onto the deck when the halyard is released.

I Assign a crew person to lower the main halyard until the reefing grommet at the tack can be placed on the hook.

leech at all times. They pass through blocks on the boom and cleat at the mast or on the cabin top. Once the sail is lowered to the reef point and the tack is secured, the reef lines are pulled in which tightens the clew. When the halyard goes up again, all 3 corners of the sail are pulled tight and a new, smaller sail is created.

Beware, if you do not get the clew point tight enough the foot will not be taut and you will have a very full, baggy mainsail. Even though there is less sail area, it may be more powerful than the

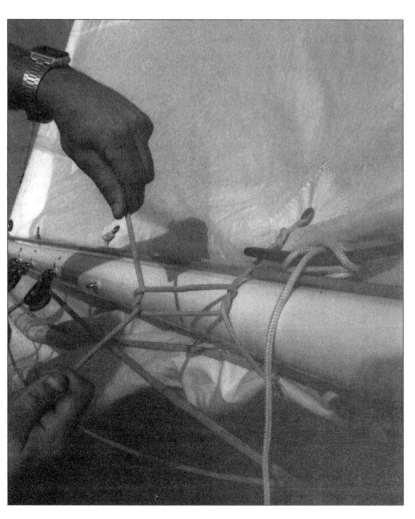

Reefing lines are used to tie up excess sail cloth. Don't hold the working part of the sail to the boom with them or you could rip the sail.

2 Have another crew person tighten the clew. Once you have pulled horizontal wrinkles along the foot of the sail, have the halyard crew tighten the main halyard.

3 Sheet in and off you go.

All the sail material we took off the mast is now drooping all over the deck and represents a lot of windage. So you must get rid of it. Traditionally, there are grommets or ties built into mainsails along the reefed foot area. If the boat has them, roll the sail neatly and tie them loosely. These grommets are not reinforced and can handle very little pressure.

Some boats have roller booms to reduce sail area. This equipment was discussed in Chapter 2. Once again, the helmsman must sail with the jib and rudder only. Release the mainsheet and allow the sail to luff. This type of sail uses a combination of halyard release and furling of the sail to reduce sail area. Use the winch handle to roll the boom, as mentioned in Chapter 2.

To shake out a reef simply get sailing with just the jib and rudder again. Take the strain off the halyard and loosen the tack and clew. Reraise the halyard to the masthead.

HEAVE–TO
Just as crew overboard exercises should be practiced in every new boat and all wind conditions, you should know what it takes for each boat to heave-to. Pick a day when winds are sustained above 15-20 knots. Use the following procedure to attempt heaving-to.

1 Prepare to tack.

2 Tack slowly, allowing boat speed

A retractable rudder comes in very handy near launch ramps and in shallow water.

to come down by staying in irons longer than usual.

3 Do not release the jib sheet. Force the jib to backwind.

4 As the wind forces the bow to leeward, push the tiller to leeward and attempt to steer back upwind.

5 Adjust the mainsheet as much as is necessary to maintain your 45-50° angle to the wind.

At this point you should be able to tell whether the boat moves forward at all. If it does, it isn't hove-to.

Next try to furl the jib and maintain the same angle using only a reefed main. This experiment should teach you a lot about your boat. Most modern trailer–able multihulls want to keep moving forward. Getting them to stop isn't easy.

There are two ways to get the boat to sail again. First, you simply release the jib from the windward side and sheet it in on the leeward side, then sheet in the main and off you go.

Or you could bear off, jibe and the jib is already set for the

heading you had taken before heaving–to.

ANCHORING
You can look at trimarans as monohulls with training wheels. While anchoring procedures won't differ much from monohulls, being lighter will make them behave a little more actively at anchor. That means they will be more quickly affected by wind, current or wave changes.

It helps to raise the boards and rudders while the boat sits at anchor. That way the boat does not try to sail around on the underwater appendages.

Remember, water passing over the uneven surfaces of boards and rudders will create lift and with enough of it the boat takes off.

With the boards up, this tendency will be highly reduced, if not eliminated.

ANCHORING/TOWING BRIDLE
Some catamarans have anchor cleats in the middle of the forward beam. Trimarans often use the bow on the main hull for

This anchoring bridle has been preset at the dock. A loop in the middle will help the boat tie securely to an anchor rode or mooring.

Anchoring procedures on multihulls differ very little from the same tasks on monohulls.

anchoring. Anchoring a multihull using either of these simple attachment points may not produce the secure experience you expect.

A bridle creates a single point, forward of the boat, to which the anchor rode can attach. The result is much more like anchoring a monohull than the other methods of attachment.

We use a line such as a portion of anchor or dock line about 150% longer than the beam. Tie a loop about 6 inches long into the middle of the line. Attach one end to each bow. Your anchor line or mooring line then attaches to the midpoint loop. This anchor bridle allows the multihull's weight to rest evenly against the anchor rode.

Imagine what would happen if you anchored a multihull from one hull. Wind and/or current would try to push the rest of the boat away from the point where the rode attached. The other hull would be pushed downwind. As the boat turned 45° away from the wind, windage on the boat and spars would act like a sail and it would begin to move forward. Eventually the anchor rode would guide it up into the wind and it would stop, only to blow back to leeward and begin the process all over again.

Boats in this condition are said to be sailing on their hulls. It makes for sleepless nights for the multihull skipper who didn't bother to learn about anchor bridles.

The same anchor bridle can be used while being towed or for towing another vessel.

GETTING SET

Most likely, trailerable multihull sailors will be working against wind and current using only an outboard motor when the time comes to anchor. Maximize maneuverability by keeping your boards down until the boat is securely anchored.

You will need to flake your anchor rode on deck and have available crew positioned on the bow, just as you would on a monohull. The rest should be simple and familiar.

1 Select a protected spot with plenty of swinging room.

2 Bring the bow to rest pointing into the wind or current, whichever is greater.

3 Have the crew lower the anchor, noting the amount of rode they let out before it hits the bottom. Having 5, 10 or 20 foot loops laid out on deck helps the measuring process.

4 With the crew still measuring, back away from the anchor spot.

5 Have the crew inform you when the rode has reached 3 or more times the distance to the bottom.

6 Crew snubs the anchor rode and the boat continues to move backward until the anchor grabs. If the anchor will not grab let out line equal to the original depth measurement and try snubbing again.

7 Once the anchor is set, continue backing away and letting out line until at least a 7:1 ratio is reached.

8 Tie the rode to the loop in your bridle and coil excess rode on deck.

ADDITIONAL ANCHORING TECHNIQUES
Mediterranean ports often have a quay which is just a bulk-

head with cleats or other attachments for dock lines. Boats use one anchor off their bow and back up to the quay. By tying tightly between a secure anchor and the bulkhead, the boat stays put and other boats can pull in alongside.

Trailerable multihulls often use a variation on this method. Instead of tying up to a quay, they maneuver into shallow water and tie their bow or stern to something on shore such as a big rock or a tree. You can also use another anchor and dig it into the sand.

Follow your standard anchoring procedure making sure you start far enough offshore to achieve 7:1 scope. Be sure to raise the boards and rudders before getting into shallow water.

CAUTION! Be sure the tide is not going out or you might be stuck there quite a bit longer than you had planned.

BEACHING
Today's multihull manufacturers often promote their products as being completely beachable. However, sailing a boat that can weigh more than a ton onto a beach should be done with great forethought.

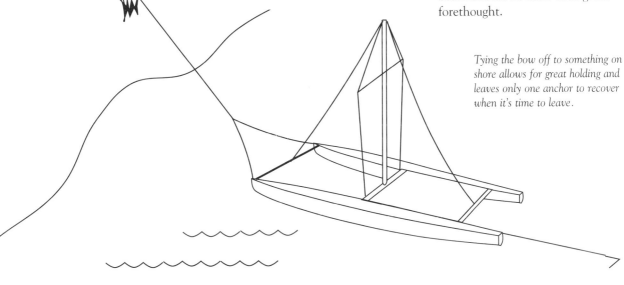

Tying the bow off to something on shore allows for great holding and leaves only one anchor to recover when it's time to leave.

As mentioned, a falling tide could make it impossible to leave until the next high tide. Rocky beaches and areas with any substantial surf should also be avoided.

As far as technique is concerned, there shouldn't be much more to it than raising the boards and easing the bows onto the sand. Your biggest concern, however, is how you will get off the beach. If you don't have a good answer to this question, don't beach the boat in the first place.

If you can immobilize the boat by putting the bows on the sand and still have enough water to back out using the engine, you're in great shape. Even in water too shallow to spin the propeller, enough muscle power will enable you to push the boat into deeper water.

Carrying an anchor out to deeper water, either by hand or in a dinghy, can also give you a means of re-floating the boat. Shifting weight to the stern and winching in the anchor line should do the trick.

Do not allow the boat to sit abeam to the shoreline. This could damage hull-mounted electronic sender units. Also, any wave action (like waverunners or powerboats stirring things up) will slam the boat from abeam and could cause damage. Try to find beaches where these vessels don't go (if that's possible).

Trailerable multihull sailors will have plenty to think about and do after learning and practicing the material in these first 4 chapters. If your interests lie in larger, cruising catamarans, there are 4 more chapters of information and exercises to explore.

GETTING ACQUAINTED

SAILING KNOWLEDGE

"The Hawaiian Kahuna, or canoe-building expert, was present at all stages of the production from the selection of the proper tree to the launching of the finished canoe. No progress could be made without his participation at each and every step, with the proper prayers and charms to ensure success."

The Island Civilizations of Polynesia
- Robert C. Suggs

NOMENCLATURE

Standing beside a cruising catamaran, especially on a floating dock which puts the boat and dock on roughly the same footing, you will probably find its size impressive. They do indeed look large. The appearance of size comes from their relatively wide beam and height off the water. Yes, there is a lot of freeboard. Some jokingly call these boats condomatamarans.

The bridge deck on smaller cats may be simply trampoline material between the hulls. Expect a rigid, fiberglass structure that rises fairly high above the hulls on a larger catamaran. This considerable height keeps the main bridge above the waves. On some of the early designs the bridge, or main deck, would get slapped by waves. While this rarely caused any damage, it interfered with sleep. Even at anchor, a wave slap often sounds like thunder.

As you look around the marina you will notice both cata-marans and trimarans in the 30 to 50 foot variety. You will recall from earlier chapters, catamarans have two hulls and trimarans have three hulls. Look closer at the two types of multihulls in this size range. Currently most production boats, meaning boats made by

attach the mainsheet to the mainsail. On these larger catamarans, there will almost always be a forward beam attached between the bows.

Main and aft beams on smaller catamarans were made of structural metal, usually some sort of tube or extruded material. They were right there in the open and their strength could be estimated by their size.

On larger catamarans you will probably not be able to see the beams quite as well. Design and construction techniques usually mold fiberglass around the actual structural material and it is not visible. You can safely assume it is under there somewhere.

Downward pressure transferred to the main beam by the mast and rigging, while considerable on a trailerable multi, becomes much greater on a bigger boat. Moderate winds and strenuous sheeting increase this downward thrust. And, by the way, expect your multihull with its high aspect ratio mainsail to need much harder sheeting than a monohull. The result of that hard sheeting is downward pressure on the mast.

Think about it. If you pull really hard on the mainsheet, force gets transferred to the sail and mast, pulling them aft and downward. The forestay and shrouds prevent the mast from being pulled aft or to either side. That added force has to go somewhere so it becomes additional downward weight on the mast.

The main beam in turn supports the additional downward pressure. All masts exert some degree of downward pressure in this manner. Monohull masts push down on the keel — a very substantial platform. Dolphin strikers, mentioned in Chapter 1, are rarely seen on larger, cruising cats.

The bridgedeck (above) spans the distance between the hulls. This dolphin striker (left) won't hit any fish because it is encapsulated within the fiberglass bridgedeck structure.

commercial companies for sale to the public, are catamarans. Virtually all the trimarans you see are project boats made by individuals in their yards or garages. Discussion of boats in Chapters 5 through 8 will, therefore, be limited to catamarans.

Once again, beams or cross members form the structural connection between the hulls. There is the main beam, the cross member where the mast is usually stepped, and an aft or rear beam, which supports the stern of the boat and normally is used to

Instead, the mast is stepped on a portion of the bridgedeck that is reinforced to take the extra force.

Let's not forget that larger catamarans usually have a third beam near the bow called the forward beam. The forestay attaches to the beam and it creates a lot of upward pressure on this span. Remember, when we're sheeted hard the forestay becomes tight and the boat can sail closer to the wind going to weather.

With the forestay attached in the middle of the forward beam, tremendous upward force would try to lift that center point. The beam itself has built-in structural integrity which can withstand the combined forces of wind and the rigging. However, on larger cats the potential upward force could be so great that the size and weight of a cross member which could withstand it would be impractical.

Use of a fabricated metal structure and cables which, together are called a seagull striker, can re-distribute the load along the forward beam. You can see from the illustration, a seagull striker takes upward pressure off the single forestay attachment point and disperses it between the points where the fabricated structure is welded to the forward beam.

This diagram of a seagull striker illustrates how the load is distributed along the forward beam.

In addition, cables stretching from the fabricated structure to the ends of the forward beam further distribute that load along the beam. Distributing the load in this manner allows for a lighter, less rigid beam and keeps some performance damaging weight off the bow.

The same results are often accomplished using a bridle, similar to those discussed in Chapter 1. Rather than placing the upward force at one center point on the forward beam, the bridle attaches to either end of the beam. Force is then distributed along the entire length of the beam.

DECKS

Catamarans have only one deck, which spans between the hulls. It can be an open deck, which uses netting or trampoline material, or it can be a closed deck and made of solid material such as fiberglass or wood. Netting or trampoline material is rarely used on large catamarans except, perhaps, between the bows. That area is forward of the

main beam and is part of the bridge deck. It can be either open and made of netting, or closed, a rigid structure. Older cats usually had closed bridge decks. Trends in new designs have recently moved toward an open bow. Netting

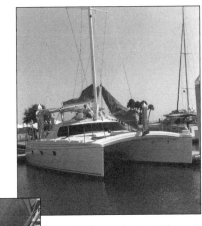

No dolphin striker is visible between the hulls of this Manta 40 (above). The forward beam closes in the bow area (left).

makes the boat lighter allowing for heavier cargo elsewhere onboard.

Taking a walk on deck from bow to stern, you will first see a foredeck that seems as large as a tennis court. As mentioned, it could be either all fiberglass or

The bow area on this catamaran has two separate trampolines.

Expansive deck space allows for ample stowage.

Work at the mast can be performed from the cabin top, which, on this boat, is accessible by steps from the foredeck.

This rigid Bimini provides shade, shelter from rain and a perfect place to mount solar panels for battery charging.

mesh tramp. There is usually plenty of room for hatches in the bow of each hull. Because it tapers to a point this area rarely gets used for living space down below. Hatches give access for storage of such things as anchors and rode, docklines and fenders. Larger cats may also have A/C electric generators in one of these spots.

This wide open bow area is a great platform for hanking on a storm sail. Foredeck crew never lean over open water and never get anywhere close to the sides of the boat. These boats offer far greater crew safety than conventional monohulls.

Some designs have a boarding ladder hinged from the forward beam with the other end held up horizontally above the water under the deck. When beaching the boat the ladder is lowered and you can walk right down to shallow water and perhaps even right onto the beach.

Moving aft you have to walk around the cabin, as you would in any boat. Notice once again the expansive deck area around the mast and boom. Without a lot of heeling, you can expect to feel pretty secure working in this area. Most cats have hatches which open to the living areas of the hulls as well as cabin top hatches over the main bridge.

Aft of the cabin you will find a huge cockpit area. Some newer designs include rigid

Bimini-type covers over the cockpit. Manufacturers feel these boats have plenty of areas where sun worshippers can pay homage. Shielding the cockpit keeps sun and light rain away from everyone else. A rigid top also prevents rapid deterioration of materials such as canvas and eliminates noise from woven material when it gets into heavier breezes.

The cockpit sits high above the water providing a very safe haven for the crew in adverse conditions. If a monohull got hit by a wave that filled the cockpit, water ballast high up in the boat would make it unstable. This cannot happen in a catamaran. Freeboard is high and the cockpit is in the middle so waves have a harder time finding the cockpit. In most cases, even if the cockpit filled with water it would still not destabilize this sturdy platform. Its wide stance and ample flotation would keep the boat sailing flat.

Most larger cats have all running rigging led to the cockpit and usually to one spot in the cockpit. This way one person can literally run the boat alone.

Aft of the cockpit you will see swim steps built right into the hulls on most modern catamarans. They make great boarding platforms for snorkelers and divers.

Catamaran cabins are usually located in each hull and across the span between the hulls. This combined space usually affords a lot more living room and comfort than most boats. The larger the cat, the easier it is to merge the cabin that spans between the hulls with the space within the hulls to make one huge inside living area.

Let's take a look at a common catamaran layout: Stepping in from the expansive cockpit brings you down below. Except in a catamaran, "below" is a misnomer. You enter on the same level as the cockpit. It isn't like going into the "basement" of your monohull.

As you enter the boat from the cockpit notice that you are not only NOT going below, you are still comfortably above the

(Top) Many sail control lines are led to one winch.
(Above) Two large swim steps keep bathers from bumping into one another on their way back aboard.

water. You can still enjoy a great panoramic view of the water. Most catamarans are very airy and open feeling. Some feature full, 360-degree visibility from inside. Contrast this with the partial view afforded most monohull sailors and you begin to understand why bigger cats have become the rage among bareboat charter customers throughout the world.

The first area you enter on most models is the main salon. "U" or crescent shaped dining areas have become quite popular on many catamarans. Some include the galley and/or nav station along the aft bulkhead. Boats with a galley in the main salon are referred to as having a "galley up" layout. Proponents of the galley up feel the cook should be sociable while preparing meals.

The navigation station may be separate or part of the salon settees. Either way, there should be plenty of room to open charts and perform plotting.

Instruments and the electrical panel may also be found in

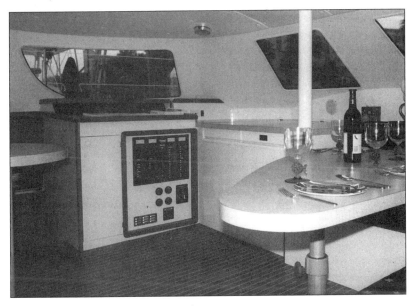

The main salon provides living space with a view.

this area. Just as you would on a monohull, examine every aspect of the electrical panel to determine which switches operate key electrical components. Does this boat have an A/C panel? If it does you may want to be on the lookout for a generator (assuming you didn't find one in the bow compartments). If the boat has A/C generating ability, some of the electrical outlets and appliances may run on A/C or D/C power. The time to figure out which type of electrical current runs which devices is now, not when you're underway or in some sort of emergency.

Interior stairs on both sides of the main salon will take you below to cabins within each hull.

The hulls are generally divided into forward, middle and aft sections. The middle section of one hull may serve as the nav sta-

tion, while the middle section of the other hull could house a galley. When the galley is located in the hull, it is referred to as "galley down." Proponents of this layout say it allows for a more open salon and keeps the disorder of meal preparation out of sight. Many modern cats use the galley down without a bulkhead between the galley and the salon. Without that barrier, a person preparing food can easily talk with crew members in the salon. So you can still have social interaction with the cook, and keep the galley mess out of sight.

The forward and aft sections are normally for private staterooms and/or head/showers.

Staterooms in catamaran hulls, especially those in aft sections can be designed with huge, king-sized beds. In these cases the bed is actually placed on the

Newcomers to multihulls will be pleasantly surprised by the ample working and storage space in the galley (top). This corner of the main salon (middle) houses the icebox, navigation station and electrical panel. Although there probably won't be many serviceable items, it's a good idea to familiarize yourself with the inside of the electrical panel (bottom).

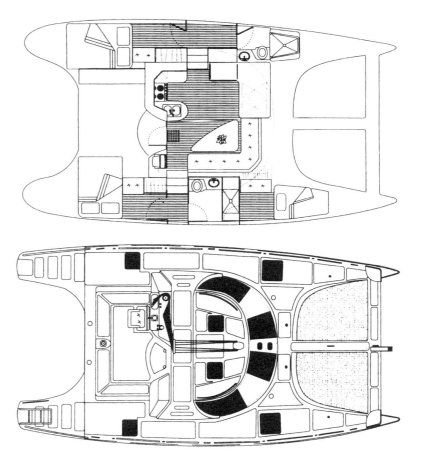

bridge area and extends over the water. This is yet another reason the bridge is built high off the waves. Even smaller cruising catamarans have lots of space relative to monohulls and trailerable multis. For example, an older O'Brien design of a 30-foot cat has two queen-sized beds in two separate staterooms, a large head with a shower, a chart room, a huge galley and vast salon, in addition, to the big, wide open aft cockpit and foredeck.

The Manta 40 makes fantastic use of all its available space. A huge deck and cockpit area allows crew members to lounge in comfort or help sail the boat with lots of elbow room. Sunbathers can even lounge on the rigid Bimini if they so desire.

Down below the main salon houses a spacious U–shaped dinette, nav station and a galley that actually allows you to cook and move around. Each hull has a double stateroom, head and storage. Monohull sailors will find it takes a while to get used to all this room in a boat that actually sails!

Automatic, electrical bilge pumps usually come as standard equipment and are located in the middle section of each hull under the floor panel. Additional pumps may be found aft in the engine compartments. Also, there are normally built in hand-operated pumps located on deck, somewhere around the cockpit, for emergency pumping when the electricity fails.

A few smaller cruising cats use single outboard engines for auxiliary power. A small minority also uses two outboards recessed into wells in the hulls. Most modern cruising catamarans use twin inboard diesel engines. They are usually mounted under some type of furniture that is easily removed,

making access to the engine fairly easy. In the photo, the engine compartment is found below a bunk. You will also find designs which permit engine access through deck hatches. As long as the engine compartment has plenty of room to work, this set-up can prevent you from having to move gear and boat parts every time you want to get down to the engine.

STABILITY

Stability is one thing trailerable multis and cruising cats have in common. Larger catamarans give you an even greater sense of steadiness than trailerable multis. Just like trailerables, cruising cats use their breadth to sail flat. Heavier displacement,

as well as more weight in gear, fuel and water all add to their stability. It takes a lot of wind to raise a hull off the water. In fact, one of the leading American multihull

Automatic bilge pumps (top) will be located in each hull. By turning the bed sideways (below) and extending it under the bridgedeck, many cruising cat designs actually include full, double berths.

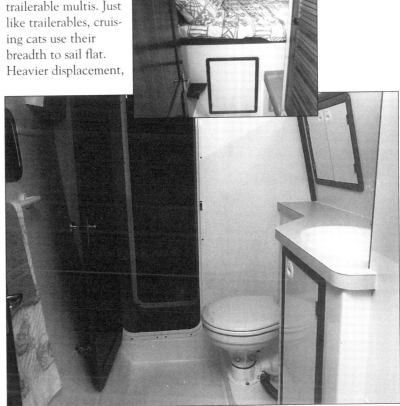

Cruising cats in the 30 to 50 foot range usually include 2 head/shower cabins.

This inboard diesel, located under a bunk in an aft stateroom, has plenty of work room on all sides. This will not always be the case.

designers, Gino Morelli, claims that the modern cruising catamaran cannot be capsized. He says it is very underpowered in its power-to-weight ratio and a person would have to almost force it to capsize.

Would you think that adding a lot of weight to any boat would be an advantage? Probably not! Weight has a price in all boats. In fact, there could be a huge list of disadvantages — the worst of those being that a heavy boat will sink faster. But in this case more weight makes the boat sturdier, easing the fears of people who can't shake the image of beach cats capsizing.

So the boat's beam keeps it sailing flat and weight makes it sturdier. In general, cruising cats have an even lower power to weight ratio than trailerables. This contributes to their inability to capsize. Consider the Manta 40 once again. It has 13,000 pounds of displacement with under 800 square feet of sail area. To put that in perspective, the Prindle 19, a beach cat people often capsize for fun, weighs 385 pounds and has a sail area of 247 square feet. A

Hunter 40.5 monohull, with roughly the same sail area as the Manta, has a displacement of 20,000 pounds.

Cruising cats, like their trailerable relatives, also have less drag. They use much slimmer hull designs than a monohull the same length. Meanwhile there is much more power-to-weight than the monohull which translates into SPEED.

So, like trailerable multihulls, cruising cats sail very flat in normal winds. When the winds pick up, monohulls heel badly telling you to reduce sail. Not so with multihulls. The boat will continue to sail flat with greater speed. Monohull sailors feel excessive heeling and a heavy helm in higher winds.

The multihull resists heeling high up in the scale of winds, and when it finally reaches the point where there is too much wind, the boat can react drastically. Flying a hull and capsizing happen despite the low probability.

Multihull sailors should think about reducing sail long before it becomes a danger. In other words, multihulls don't tell the sailor when they are overpowered. It takes intuition borne of experience.

Comparative stability curves show how multihulls fight the tendency to heel better than monohulls. You'll have to get used to very little heeling, no rolling tendency and associated steering problems (such as heavy weather helm) and more sail-carrying ability. Unless you like going slow, working hard and getting knocked around, that should come as welcome news.

AUXILIARY POWER OPTION

Let's consider the outboard engine. While it is less expensive to purchase than an inboard engine, it costs much more through its inefficiency. Outboards use a lot more fuel per mile than diesel engines. The big advantage of outboards is that they

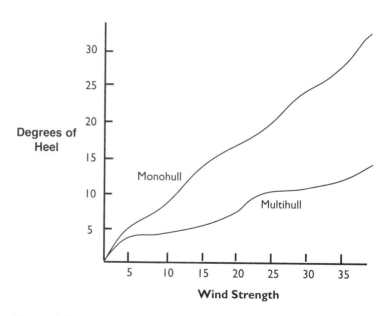

This graph illustrates the difference between monohull and multihull heeling angles in freshening breezes.

can be lifted from the water while sailing, thereby reducing drag. However, storing gasoline on a boat creates potential hazards most boat owners choose to avoid.

Inboard gas engines, which were once popular on cruising boats, have all but disappeared on cruising cats. Gas leaks, which are much more likely to occur on carburetor-fed gas engines, can cause disastrous explosions and fires. Outboard gas engines which are not contained in a well or compartment are the exception to this rule. If it experiences a leak, an uncontained outboard simply drips gas into the water or on the boat.

With an inboard gas engine leaked fuel goes into the engine compartment and bilge where it can vaporize in the presence of large amounts of oxygen. With enough fuel and oxygen a stray spark can turn a boat into a pyrotechnic display.

Outboards also experience cavitation, a problem that doesn't plague inboard diesels. Cavitation describes the condition that occurs when the propeller turns but it pushes air rather than water. This happens when the prop gets too near the surface of the water.

Let's say we are motoring along and Rodney Dangerfield comes by on his 45' Hatteras at full throttle. "No respect!" Our stern-mounted engines rise and fall with the waves. As soon as we rock high enough — zingo! — cavitation.

With cavitation comes the alarming scream of the engines, as their RPMs skyrocket. Then they catch the water again. Next time they go airborne you hear more screaming RPMs. It's your engine's way of telling you it isn't happy.

A strut-mounted, folding prop keeps drag to a minimum under sail.

This catamaran uses two outboards for power. Under sail they can tip up and eliminate drag from shafts and propellers altogether.

But, how often does Rodney come around? Heck, we can live with a little boat chop once in a while. But what if you were trying to motor into Cape Fear River (North Carolina) with an ebb tide and an onshore breeze. There would be huge, standing waves in those conditions. The cavitation phenomenon would be horrible. You would not be making much headway and you may end up ruining the engines.

Outboards are usually much more unreliable and they have a short life expectancy compared to diesel engines.

Another big consideration is D/C electricity. Operating all the goodies on larger multihulls takes a lot of it. You have all that nav gear, lights, refrigeration, etc. all needing juice. Outboards come with very small-output alternators.

They normally put out just enough power to charge their own starting battery. They are not designed to keep a large boat operating. Alternative electricity generation would have to be added for any serious cruising on a catamaran with outboard engines.

Diesels seem to be the best choice, even though they add considerable weight to the boat.

They can be set up with power take-offs to run refrigeration, air conditioning, and charge up massive battery banks. Electrical capabilities, fuel consumption, reliability and safety make diesel the engine-of-choice for cruising cats.

Now, how do we put this power to the water? Most large multihulls use conventional shafting and fixed-blade propellers.

This set-up adds drag because of the fixed props and shafts protruding below the hull. These underwater appendages also reduce the boat's ability to get into shallow water or beaches, unless they are protected.

Some boat owners choose folding props because they reduce a lot of the drag. But folding props are expensive and have been

---

YOU WILL NEED TO START YOUR DIESEL ENGINES TO PERFORM THE SAILING SKILLS EXERCISES IN THIS CHAPTER. FOLLOW THESE STEPS TO GET THEM STARTED.

1 Determine whether the auxiliary engine runs on gasoline or diesel fuel. Deck fillers may give a clue but they could be wrong. An owner's manual, if available, will provide fairly reliable information.

2 Locate the main battery switch down below and turn it to "All" or "Both." This sends battery power to the starter and blower.

3 Locate the "Blower" or "Bilge Blower" switch either on the main switch panel or the engine control panel in the cockpit. Turn it on. Let it run for five minutes. Gasoline fumes are heavier than air and extremely combustible. A bilge blower, which acts as an exhaust fan for the bilge, must be operated for at least five minutes prior to starting the engine. Diesel fumes are much less volatile but, if gasoline for the outboard and/or liquefied petroleum gas for the galley stove are present, dangerous fumes could still settle in the bilge. Always run the blower before starting the engine.

4 Verify that the gear shift is in neutral. The gear shift snaps gently into and out of gear while the throttle travels from the slowest setting to the fastest setting with uniform resistance. Finding neutral should be easy after pushing the shift and throttle all the way forward and back a few times.

If two separate levers are not present for the throttle and shift, a single lever Morse Control system could be mounted in the cockpit. It consists of a lever and a button. The lever acts only as a throttle when the button is out (or in, it varies and you must determine which is correct). The transmission stays in neutral. Push the button in and the lever controls both shifting and engine speed. Perform the "Gear

check" described in SAILING SKILLS to clarify the button and lever functions.

5 Set the throttle about halfway between where it stops in both directions.

6 Locate the engine fuel shut-off lever. There may be a small handle which pulls out and pushes back in. Look around the engine control panel or in the lazarette. It must be pushed in before the engine will start.

7 Locate the "Glow Plug" or pre-heater if the engine comes equipped with one. It may have its own switch or it may work by turning the key in one direction or the other. It probably needs the key turned "on," one click to the right, if it has a separate switch. When the key goes to the "on" position a buzzer should sound. It indicates that either cooling water is not flowing or oil pressure has dropped. We accept both conditions from an engine before it has started. 20 seconds seems to be the standard prescription for glow plug operating time.

8 Start the engine. Either operate the starter by turning the key beyond "on," like a car, or by pressing a separate button near the key. Stand by to back off the throttle in case the engine races.

If the engine fails to start after a few tries of less than 10 seconds each, try advancing the throttle. Otherwise, repeat steps 7 and 8. Avoid cranking the engine excessively. If it will not start, then something substantial is wrong. Have it checked out by a mechanic.

known to fail at just the wrong time, while approaching a dock and reversing engines to stop, for example.

Some designers have experimented with jet-drives similar to those on jet-skis while others have tried inboard-outboard type outdrives.

Jet drives sound like a good choice, offering the ability to get into shallow waters without fear of damage and less drag while under sail. However, critics claim that jet drives are very inefficient, particularly in lower horse-powered engines.

Locate all through-hulls prior to sailing

Outdrives on powerboats have been a maintenance nightmare over the years. There's no reason to believe this would change when you put them on sailboats. Their best feature is an ability to be pulled up while under sail thus reducing drag. Catamarans can opt for an engine in each hull, or a single engine mounted in a pod below the middle of the deck.

If you have just one engine (whose prop usually goes in the water between the hulls), boat handling will be a little precarious. You only have one source of thrust much like you would with an outboard engine on a trailerable. While this arrangement works just fine on small multihulls, you may not have adequate control on larger boats with a lot of windage. Without pushing water across a rudder your boat may loose maneuvering capabilities, especially at slow speeds.

A number of boats utilize single engines with propellers in each hull. They have separate hydraulic drives and transmissions for each prop. This gives you excellent handling ability in close quarters. Since they are outdrives, they can be raised while sailing for drag reduction. One engine is lighter than two, and much less expensive. Multihulls in the 35+ foot range invariably use two engines, one in each hull. It certainly adds weight and expense to the boat, but the advantages justify the expense. For offshore cruising two engines increase safety and comfort. You have two alternators creating electricity and you can conserve fuel by using only one engine when speed and maneuverability aren't essential. With two engines in close quarters you have a boat that handles like a pussy cat.

Engine sizes depend on the boat, its length and its weight. Obviously, the bigger the boat and the more amenities it has to run, the more power you'll need from your engine(s). The good news is that diesel engines are getting more powerful and lighter, exactly what catamaran designers need to add value to their products.

Here's what you see looking forward from the helm of a 40 foot cruising catamaran.

With two engines and a generator there may be more battery switches and batteries than you are used to seeing.

As is the case with all bigger boats, control panels have more to control.

Since catamarans have the ability to go fast, sailors have come to expect speed under power or sail. That hasn't always been the case. Designers of the last generation of cruising cats often subscribed to the theory that motoring any sailboat was a slow process.

Today's designers are more likely to install light, powerful, high-rpm diesels which help their boats reach speeds of 7-10 knots while under power.

SEE APPENDIX A FOR SAILING KNOWLEDGE QUIZ

SAILING SKILLS

Let's get ready to cast off a dock. You probably won't find yourself leaving a slip very often. Most marinas do not have slips wide enough to accommodate the beam of a cruising cat. So this exercise will run through casting-off with our port side to a dock.

First, make a thorough check of the boat, making sure to locate every through-hull fitting. Check each valve to ensure it is free and working properly. Make sure engine intakes are open. Check for compliance with all government regulations, safety equipment, ship's papers and registrations. Shore power should be turned off and disconnected prior to starting the engines.

Most of the information in this exercise will focus on boats with two diesel engines. All exercises should be performed regardless of your boat's engine configuration. The results will differ but a great deal of learning can occur as a result of experimentation. Always leave yourself plenty of sea room for maneuvering under power. Avoid any tendency to apply speed in closed quarters. Have crew onboard ready to fend off and place fenders between your boat and any solid obstruction it might encounter.

ENGINE STARTING

The inboard engine was arguably the most important innovation in sailing history. Purists who regard it as a noisy little nuisance usually soften their stand when presented with the alternative of sailing in and out of the harbor. The calming elixir of travel by sail can turn to unrelenting annoyance while sitting becalmed for hours on end. The inboard auxiliary engine saves us from our-

selves in such cases. It also gives sailors the option of maintaining a schedule if they so desire.

See step–by–step engine–starting instructions on previous page.

The buzzer should stop within seconds after the engine comes to life. Take a look at the gauges on the control panel. The ammeter should stand somewhere around 12 to 14 volts if the battery is charging. The water temperature gauge should point to the lowest level and can rise as far as 200°-210° without cause for alarm. Oil pressure of 40-80 pounds per square inch is fine. Once the engine has started, check the exhaust discharge to make sure that water flows out with the exhaust. This indicates that cooling water is flowing through the engine. If exhaust smoke escapes without water, turn the engine off immediately. Something is very wrong.

A good battery will register 12 volts or slightly above 12 volts.

Repeat the starting procedure for the other engine.

Now that the engines are up and running smoothly, it's time to check out the steering and the gears. First turn the wheel to the left until it stops. Now turn right until it stops again. Count the number of full turns. Divide that number in half, and turn back that many turns. Wrap some colored plastic tape around the wheel or a spoke at the top. Whenever you are within one turn of half (if the wheel turned 3 times it would be turn #2) and the tape lines up on top, your rudders, outboard(s) or outdrive(s) are centered.

For example, if you turned a total of 3 turns from lock to lock, the tape will be at the top 3 times. Obviously, when the wheel locks on one side or the other with the tape on top, it isn't centered. So the only turn where the tape matters is the middle turn. For the time being, let's keep the tape at the top and the rudders centered.

Now, let's check out the gear shift(s). With the engine at idle speed put the starboard gear into forward. Notice the dock lines. The bow line and the stern springline should both go slack, while the bow spring and stern line will get taut. As soon as you see that, pull the gear shift back to neutral. Now you should see the boat rock back and forth on the dock lines and eventually settle down to its original position. Do the same with the port engine.

Next, let's check reverse. Pull the starboard gear shift into reverse. The bow spring and the stern line should go slack, while the aft spring and bow line get taut. Again, put the gear shift back to neutral and check the results. Do the same with the port engine.

Gearshifts in these positions would cause the propellers to work against each other. The result would be a severe turn to the left which would resemble counter-clockwise rotation more than a turn.

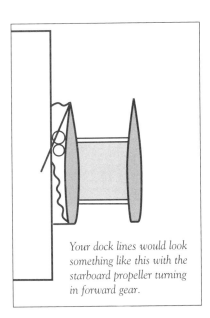

Your dock lines would look something like this with the starboard propeller turning in forward gear.

This test will be roughly the same for any boat with a propeller in each hull.

This quick check elimi-nates any guessing about which way the gear shifts move. Some boats reverse the shifting direction and it may be the opposite of what you expect. A few minutes at the dock can eliminate mistakes and possible damage to your boat or someone else's.

At this point it would also be a good idea to check the rotation of the props. Are they both turning the same way? Manufacturers often configure gears to turn props in opposite directions. This neutralizes prop walk when both props are spinning in forward or reverse.

A single outboard engine located somewhere between the hulls will probably not cause the boat to move very much as a result of prop walk. As mentioned earlier, outboards tend to have less lateral thrust. In addition, the cat's waterline, which is twice that of a comparable monohull, will resist prop walk motion.

Let's eliminate more guess work. We want to check the forces working on our boat while sitting here on the dock. Two external forces, wind and current, can affect our departure from this dock.

First take a look at the most obvious, the wind. Look at the wind indicators on your boat — electronic wind indicators, perhaps, a masthead fly, or just yarn or cassette tape on the shrouds. Which direction is the wind blowing? If it comes from the dock and blows toward the water, the wind will help you. If the wind is blowing from the water onto the dock, it's going to cause you some problems.

Any strong tendency for the stern to get pulled in one direction or the other while making forward way is neutralized when propellers turn in opposite directions going forward.

But wind is not the only factor. Often, and particularly in big tidal areas, the current has as much or more effect on boat handling.

The best way to check is to just look down at the water and see which way it is moving. Reading bubbles, debris or anything floating in the water as it goes by will give you the answer. Toss a single cracker into the water if you can't tell otherwise. It isn't littering. Fish and seagulls will thank you.

So, which is the stronger — wind or current?

For this first attempt, assume you have decided the wind is on the nose and current is not a problem. You have only two line handlers, so let's get them oriented. If you look at the dock lines, you will probably see that the bow spring and the stern line are slack, while the bow and the stern spring are taut. That's what happens with the wind on the nose trying to push the boat backward.

1 Appoint a bowline person and a stern line person.

2 Have them take off the slack lines. After all, the lines are not doing anything anyway.

3 Have the stern line person tie one end of a clean line (no knots) to the stern cleat. Run it once around a dock cleat or piling forward of the boat's stern cleat opposite the beam. This is referred to as a "running line." It takes the place of the stern springline. Make sure the line is long enough to extend back to the line handler on deck.

4 Remove the stern springline.

5 Be sure the stern of the boat is well fendered.

6 Have the bow person remove the bowline. Wind blowing on the

Crew stands by, ready to cast off this running springline on captain's command.

bow with the running line still secure should make the bow swing to seaward. If not, you can help it.

7 Pull the starboard gear shift into reverse. The rear thrust of the outside engine will pull the bow well off the dock.

8 Now that the bow is clear and heading in the proper direction, say 30 to 45 degrees off the dock, put both engines in forward.

9 Have the stern line person pull the running line from the deck cleat and toss the running end toward the piling or cleat. Remember that we had the helm straight and now the boat will move away from the dock cleanly.

CASTING-OFF WITH A STERN WIND

1 Appoint a bowline person and a stern line person.

2 Have them take off the slack lines. In this case it should be the bowline and stern spring.

3 Have the bowline person tie one end of a running line to the bow cleat. Run it once around a dock cleat or piling well aft of the boat's bow cleat in the beam area. Make sure the line is long enough to extend back to the line person on deck.

4 Remove the bow springline.

5 Be sure the bow of the boat is well fendered.

6 Have the stern person remove the stern line. Wind blowing on the stern with the running line still secure should make the stern swing to seaward. If not, you can help it.

7 Pull the port gear shift into reverse. The rear thrust of the inside engine will pull the stern well off the dock.

8 Now that the stern is clear and heading into open water, put both engines in reverse.

9 Have the bowline person pull the running line from the deck cleat and toss the running end toward the piling or cleat. Remember that we had the helm straight and now the boat will move away from the dock cleanly.

CASTING-OFF WITH A STRONG BUT FAVORABLE WIND

If the wind blows off the dock, you can expect fewer problems. You could use either of the above techniques or simply remove the springlines then the bow – and stern lines.

Most of the time you want to take your dock lines with you. Removing one running line last allows you to do just that. Casting-off in a wind that blows

you off the dock is easy in light winds. Your crew can stand on the dock and manhandle the boat long enough to get onboard. In higher winds, you may need a running line.

1 Attach your running line to a midship cleat. Run it forward or aft to a dock cleat or piling.

2 Use your inside (closer to the dock) engine to either back down on a line led forward or run forward against a line led aft.

The onboard line handler will need to keep tension on the running line.

3 Have crew on the dock remove dock lines as they become slack.

4 Dock crew boards boat.

5 Gear is shifted to neutral.

6 Onboard crew slips running line off dock cleat or piling and pulls it

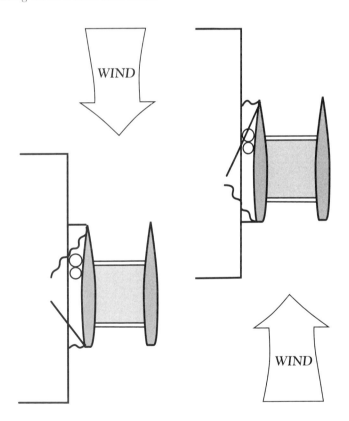

Wind from the bow or stern makes it easy to decide which dock lines to remove first.

Fewer hull marks and scrapes occur when dock-side adjustments are done by hand (above) instead of using engine power. When help just isn't available, a good plan will get the job done (below).

aboard.

7 Helmsperson can either allow the wind to blow the boat free, using engines to adjust for angle changes, or use one of the methods described above.

LEAVING A DOCK WITH WIND BLOWING YOU ONTO IT

The toughest dock to leave is one where the wind is blowing you onto it.

1 Remove unnecessary lines.

2 Have the bow crew put good fenders near the bow.

3 Set up a running bow spring–line. Then, instruct the stern line crew to remove lines.

4 Turn the helm to full left rudder, and put the starboard engine in forward gear.

You may have to give the engine more throttle, depending upon the wind strength. With resistance from the running spring line, the bow should press against the dock and the stern should pull away from the dock.

5 Once the stern is well off the dock, reverse both engines and straighten the rudder. Depending upon the wind strength, you may need more or less reverse throttle.

When current and wind are both present, you must determine what net result both forces will have on the boat. Strain on dock lines is probably your best indicator. Treat the combined force as if it was only wind.

CHAPTER 6
GETTING STARTED

SAILING KNOWLEDGE

"An even more effective stabilizer was made by lashing a second canoe alongside, joined to the first by booms and serving as a balance–the original catamaran. These stabilizers were termed outriggers. It was possible to erect a plank deck and an elementary cabin superstructure over the double canoe."

Pacific Voyages
- John Gilbert

Even if you don't become one yourself, you may have occasion to meet and talk to multihull zealots. A typical explanation of their choice of multiple hulled boats might include some of the following arguments.

Do you want a boat that can easily make up to 100 miles per day or one that struggles to make 50 miles per day? Would you like to moor in shallow, quiet coves away from the crowded, deep harbors or be confined to highly populated mooring sites? Would you prefer a boat that can be beached so you can swim and frolic in the sun, or one that needs to be anchored well off shore requiring a dinghy for transport to the beach?

Which would you prefer: a boat with wide open, level decks that stays flat in all wind and wave conditions, or one that has small, steeply angled, congested decks most of the time? Would you pick

a boat that has a free-feeling, open cabin or one where the cabin feels like a root cellar?

These heavily biased comparisons can get even more severe, but you get the picture. While most monohull sailors will never spend any significant amount of time on a multihull, most multihull sailors have been monohull sailors and consider the monohull world a part of their distant past.

During my younger years my wife and I used to do yacht deliveries. We were contracted to deliver a Hans Christian 38 from Norfolk, Virginia, to Key West, Florida. Since we were in no rush, and we always try to stay away from the ocean area around Cape Hatteras, we headed down the Intracoastal Waterway. The trip was uneventful until we came to Cape Fear Inlet.

It was right after Hurricane Hugo had devastated the Carolinas and very few of the bridges were operating. So we had no choice but to go out into the ocean.

The weather was fine and the winds light for the first twelve hours, and although we were fairly comfortable, we were making very poor time, even motor sailing. The winds and waves picked up. We still were not making very good time, however, and the boat was becoming very uncomfortable.

After 72 hours we were still off the Georgia coast and getting beat-up pretty badly. Neither of us could sleep. We took turns strapping ourselves into the quarter berth, but the jostling and pounding prevented any serious sleep. As we got closer to Florida we were totally exhausted. And we were starving — the refrigerator opened in the traditional way (rather than top loading) and was on the port side. So, if you opened the door on a port tack, all the food came pouring out at you with no way of getting it back in.

My wife was due to come on deck for her watch after a sleepless off-watch. She strapped herself into the galley area and began making coffee. Finally, after getting the cup of coffee just the way she liked it, she set it down for just a second to unstrap herself from the galley. Bang! A wave hit us on the beam and sent the coffee flying.

She looked up at me and screamed, "This is the last monohull I am ever going to deliver!"

BASIC CONCEPTS OF MULTIHULLS AND PERFORMANCE FEATURES

Cruising loses some of its joy when the crew becomes fatigued. It is exhausting to sail for long days and nights with a boat laying on its side and pounding through seas. That is when mistakes start happening — the crew is unable to think clearly or react quickly.

One compelling multihull virtue is its comfort factor. The boat is never heeled over and it slices nicely through the seas. This gives the crew a chance to walk around, sleep, eat and generally enjoy the ride. A comfortable ride keeps the crew rested and ready.

Ever try to navigate in heavy seas? Shoot the sun, the moon, some stars and then go below, compile and calculate all that information — with the boat bouncing around and heeled over? It's all you can do to hang on, let alone use a calculator or look up huge numbers in books.

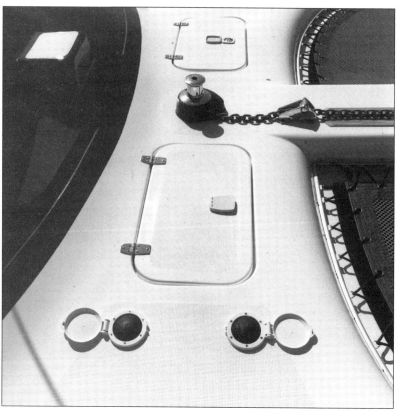

These nacelle lockers offer stowage and access to anchor rode and windlass.

Navigation in multihulls is much simpler, less tiring, and, therefore, more accurate — a great safety benefit.

SHIP'S SYSTEMS, THE COCKPIT & DECK AREA

Let's take a closer look at the boat's equipment. Most modern cruising cats have opted away from the full deck and now offer trampoline areas forward, usually with a nacelle middle bow. The nacelle is a molded fiberglass structure which protrudes below the deck. It softens the impact of waves generated by the hulls traveling through the water. It can be forward in the forward beam area or under the bridge where it can add living and stowage space.

Many cruising cats cut a hatch into the middle of the nacelle. It is a good place to stow anchors and rode and to mount a windlass.

The deck hatches on the main hull decks offer excellent storage for spare line and fenders.

Cockpits on most cruising cats are huge and roomy, like everything else. Many have a helm set up for each side of the boat providing good visibility over the cabin top and the ability to steer from a position close to the dock during docking and undocking. Dual steering stations also allow the helmsperson to see all corners of the boat and around all sails.

The cockpit is usually set up so that all the sheets and halyards feed to one spot. This enables a sailor to single-hand a very large boat. Larger multihulls have enough room to include a dedicated winch for every halyard and sheet. However, the need to be weight conscious still exists.

So, you may have a lot of sheets and halyards set up to feed

Mainsail control lines all lead neatly through turning blocks to a single winch.

one winch. Most will probably go through a stopper or clutch. That allows the sheet or halyard to be winched to the point you want it set. The clutch holds it, freeing the winch for another use.

SAILPLANS

Since the boat is light (relative to ballasted monohulls) and its speed through the water is not as restricted a lot more and varied sails can be used.

RIGS

Fractional sloop rigs are as popular with cruising cat manufacturers as they are with the makers of trailerable multihulls. A fractional rig brings with it a smaller fore triangle and a foresail with less area. The masthead sloop has not been a popular rig because of its large genoa/jib and added difficulty tacking and jibing.

Hardly any boats use split rigs (yawls or ketches) and cutter rigs. As stated in earlier chapters, they are very inefficient. They don't go to weather, they don't sail well downwind, and they only perform well on reaches. So, why pay more for an additional mast, all those extra stays and extra sails and still have a very poor sailing boat? Obviously there is no good reason.

Cruising cats usually use high aspect ratio mainsails for all the same reasons and with all the same results as their trailerable cousins. Roachy leaches and full battens are also prevalent among cruising cats. Fully battened jibs have also found their way into the world of cruising multihulls. Their added speed and efficiency make them a natural addition to this fast and efficient breed of boats.

The fractional rig mast has a few extra struts to help distribute the load.

ciency of high aspect ratio boards, it has proven a winner for cruisers and charter fleets. Designers add a 1 to 2 foot keel near the fore-and-aft center of the hulls. This lowers the center of lateral resistance which helps resist leeway.

Monohull keels perform a dual function, resist leeway and hold ballast. Stubby keels on multihulls only need to resist leeway although they do add ballast which adds stability. But like all weight on boats, it reduces performance.

In still another contrast the monohull heels over in high winds. As heel increases, the keel no longer points straight down. Tracking through the water at an angle, less of its flat area resists leeway. It loses much of its efficiency. The catamaran will still ride straight up and down in similar conditions and the keel will remain efficient.

Keels are a sacrifice, regardless of the type of boat. You give up speed for stability and draft for pointing ability no matter how you look at it. Now that big catamaran will no longer be able to get right up on the beach. You will probably end up in two feet of water. Not bad when you consider your monohull friends will need at least six or seven. It probably won't seem like too much of an inconvenience as you wade to shore and walk back and forth at will to get your things.

TACKING AND TURNING

Due to its extremely long, slim water line the catamaran likes to go straight. It's not too happy about turning. Catamaran sailors may choose to use their sails to augment the steering forces of their rudders.

Catamarans with daggerboards or centerboards need less help from the sails. Boats with

The remaining sails and running rigging will not differ substantially from what you found on the trailerable. On the cruising cat it all tends to be bigger and there's more of it. Take time to acclimate yourself to this new environment.

DAGGERBOARDS AND CENTERBOARDS

Just like everything else on bigger boats, expect these underwater appendages to be bigger and harder to handle. As a result, boats that have them usually have some sort of mechanical device to make raising and lowering boards easier. It may be lines with blocks and cleats, a winch or some sort of hand–operated windlass. If you're sailing a boat with mechanically operated boards, learn them at the dock and find out if they have any quirky raising or lowering characteristics before setting sail.

If you are chartering a large cat in the Caribbean, you will probably not have to worry about boards — most of them use a shallow, shoal-draft keel. While the shoal-draft keel lacks the effi-

boards tack much easier than those with keels. Anyone who has seen hydroplane races has witnessed an effect similar to what happens when a cat without boards turns. When hydroplanes go into a turn the angle of the boat turns long before the boat itself turns. Momentum from thrust that kept the boat tracking on the first course wants to keep it moving along that line. The boat turns and the angle of its thrust turns. There is a lag time between when the boat turns and when it begins tracking forward on the new course. The result is a wide, inefficient, arcing turn.

The same thing happens on a catamaran when thrust is redirected without leeway–resisting centerboards or daggerboards.

TURNING UNDER POWER

Nothing beats a twin engine catamaran for turning within its own length. I owned a 42' Solaris Catamaran and kept it at my dock in a canal that was only 50 feet wide. Without lines, and purely through the use of engines, I could do a 360-degree turn. This left only about a foot or so on each end, but it was plenty. Twin engines more than compensate for the catamaran's resistance to turning. Exercises in Sailing Skills will further explore this phenomenon.

TYING TO A DOCK

If you are docking in a tidal area, without floating docks

that ride up and down with the tides, you will need to allow for the tidal range.

A multihull's wide beam allows you to use long lines. Longer lines stretch more and that stretch helps keep the boat in roughly the same spot throughout the tidal rise and fall. Angling lines, rather than tying directly to the dock, can help compensate for tides. You may also need to tie lines slightly looser than you might otherwise. The worst thing you can do is tie short, straight lines very tight.

Tides often come with discernible currents, even in marinas. Although you secure your boat in the conditions present at docking time, it may ultimately get affected by current from a different direction or directions. Placement

of fenders can change dramatically with even minor boat movements. This is especially troublesome with pilings. Once the fenders no longer stand between the boat and hard spots around it, costly damage can occur very quickly. Fender boards, large spherical fenders and tying cylinder shaped fenders horizontally can help prevent damage.

> SEE APPENDIX A FOR SAILING KNOWLEDGE QUIZ

SAILING SKILLS

MANEUVERING

Docking and undocking in the last chapter allowed you to re-familiarize yourself with prop-walk. These are forces other than forward or reverse propulsion caused by propellers.

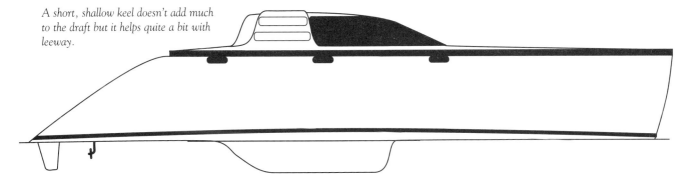

A short, shallow keel doesn't add much to the draft but it helps quite a bit with leeway.

If you had an engine quit while underway it would not be a major problem. When the boat is underway and the hulls are tracking, thrust from only one side will not turn the boat too much. With momentum, the engine is maintaining speed rather than applying force to create motion. In fact, you can save fuel by cruising with only one engine.

Taking off in forward from a dead stop is a different story. The single engine thrust will try to turn the boat toward the opposite side. For instance, if the port engine alone is propelling you forward, the boat wants to turn to the right. This problem can be corrected by rudder angle but not until the boat begins to gain speed and tracks in a straighter line due to that speed.

The opposite effect is felt in reverse. If the same starboard engine was inoperative, the bow would tend to turn to the left in reverse.

Centerboards and daggerboards will help, but not until water flows across them. So, you still have a similar problem with or without the boards.

Keeping a light hand on the throttle will minimize adverse propeller forces while getting underway. Take off slowly. As

momentum increases, so can the RPMs. Keep the momentum and throttle interactive until you get up to cruising speed.

Stopping creates the same problem with opposite effects. Using lots of reverse thrust on your port engine would not necessarily stop the boat. Most likely, it would turn to port. So operating with a single engine would require you to reduce speed and stop gradually. A little reverse thrust will probably do the trick.

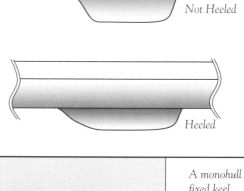

Not Heeled

Heeled

A monohull fixed keel loses some of its leeway-resisting area when the boat heels.

Using the information about what happens when thrust is applied from a single engine, imagine how well the boat would turn and generally perform with two turning propellers. For example, if you want to turn sharply to port, reversing the port engine will make it happen. Forward thrust on the starboard engine would also make the boat turn to port. So you would be absolutely correct if you assumed the combination of both port-turning forces would have a tremendous effect on a left turn. In fact, using one engine in forward and the other in reverse will allow the boat to turn in its own length.

Should either engine be configured to blow prop wash across the rudder, you gain yet another turning force. By turning the helm hard to port, water jetting back from the starboard prop would hit the rudder and help the boat turn to port.

Let's make another supposition. What if your rudders were

Long dock lines allow for rise and fall of the tides.

inoperative? With twin engines you can steer the boat effortlessly without them. In fact, it is usually best to dock with the helm centered and use the engines to control steering.

Always avoid any temptation to increase RPMs in close quarters. Have your crew ready to drop a fender between your boat and any obstruction or push off by hand. Both of these defensive moves are easier when the boat is barely moving.

PRACTICE MAKES PERFECT

Pick a spot in open water and spend lots of time experimenting with the various directions of thrust, alone and combined. Use the rudders and see how they

UNDERSTANDING TWIN SCREWS

Put an empty box on the floor. Put one finger at a point approximately halfway between the left and right edges. Try to push it. With a little balancing and adjusting, you should be able to move the box forward. Now move your finger to the outside, perhaps 1 or 2 inches from the edge. Push again and you will see the box turn to the opposite side. Put the same finger of the other hand at a spot opposite the first finger. Pushing with both fingers moves the box forward without turning. Push a little less with one finger and the box turns to that side. That's all there is to basic twin screw maneuvering, pushing (or pulling) from one side or the other.

Under full sail in a brisk breeze, the windward hull rides slightly higher than the leeward hull.

affect your turns. Increase and reduce RPMs. Generally, get the feel of twin screws and become comfortable with the options they create.

Then, get a little closer to boats, docks and pilings. It is important to get a feel for the boat's length and how short or long a distance it needs to turn. This process may be best repeated and comprehended over the course of a few days. Even though the turning and maneuvering capabilities of a cruising cat under power surpass any sailboat you may have encountered to date, another engine adds a level of complication to the process. Give yourself enough time to become comfortable with all that is new.

Stopping at a Fixed Marker Upwind Exercise

First, let's throw a marker in the water and practice motoring

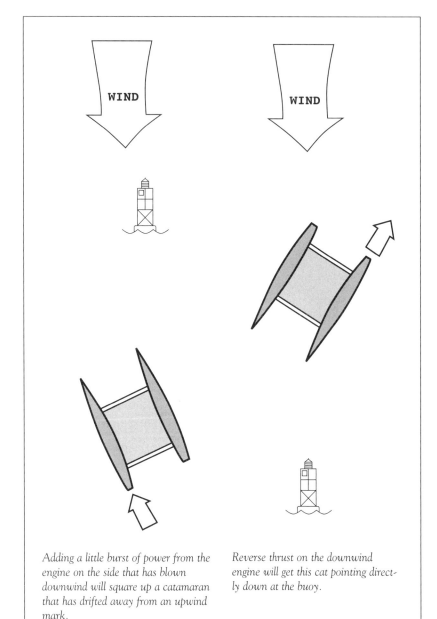

Adding a little burst of power from the engine on the side that has blown downwind will square up a catamaran that has drifted away from an upwind mark.

Reverse thrust on the downwind engine will get this cat pointing directly down at the buoy.

our multihull. We'll attempt to stop the boat within four feet of the marker. You will probably find that the boat maneuvers much easier with the centerboard or daggerboards down. This gives the boat an axis on which to turn.

Trailerables stopped easily on an upwind approach and so will cruising cats. It will require much less reverse engine thrust to slow the boat because the wind will help. Despite the extra assistance you should still approach slowly.

The bow will want to blow off to either side. This is an exercise in which the dual engine, cruising cat really shows its stuff. Going forward, apply more throttle to the engine on whichever side the boat tends to drift toward. In reverse, speed up the engine on the opposite side. Once your original course has been regained, ease off the throttle and go to neutral.

The last exercise helped point out the fact that engine thrust was a much more accurate means of maneuvering in tight quarters than rudder adjustment. Leave the helm in the neutral position for this exercise.

Once the boat has stopped altogether, you will need to use the propellers in opposite directions to maintain your position. Using one propeller or the other when trying to remain in one spot will result in a net forward or reverse thrust (whichever you used). When one engine pushes forward and the other pushes back, fore and aft thrust is canceled out. However, the wind which we determined was coming from the bow will cause you to use a little forward thrust.

Downwind Stopping Exercise

Stopping downwind calls for an even slower approach since the wind is pushing you toward your destination. Keep in mind that propeller design maximizes forward engine thrust to the disadvantage of reverse power. So, start early with reverse thrust and be ready to apply more power if necessary.

Once again, holding the bow straight downwind is much easier than holding the bow into the wind. One force at work keeping your stern pointed upwind is rudder and prop drag. When the wind starts blowing the boat downwind these underwater appendages create resistance. In so doing, they cause the stern to move slower so the bow ends up going downwind first. It has less resistance.

You want to approach

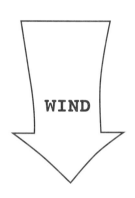

SHIFTING CAUTION

It is never advisable to shift quickly from forward to reverse. When the boat is traveling at moderate or high speeds it is even more important to avoid this practice. Propellers don't stop spinning just because you reduce speed or shift to neutral. Whenever you shift between forward and reverse, reduce RPMs to idle and allow the shift to rest in neutral for at least 5 seconds. Shifting to neutral before it is necessary and waiting longer than 5 seconds is a better practice.

very slowly. At two or three boat lengths from the mark, shift to reverse. Notice how much or little the boat slows immediately. Add more reverse power if necessary until you can see that it will slow to a stop within the available space. If you find yourself bringing the RPMs up to say, 1500-2000, you may have begun your approach too close to the marker or you were going too fast. In this case, bail out, go around and correct the approach until it works the way it should.

Stop the boat about a boat length away. Allow the boat

By "crabbing" slightly into the wind this cat can reach the intended mark.

to drift downwind a little, then shift back to reverse. This is a great way to build confidence in your stopping ability, something prudent sailors need to have.

CROSS-WIND STOPPING EXERCISE
Remember "crabbing" from Chapter 2? It comes into play in cross-wind approaches on cruising cats too, but it's easier to control.

With the wind blowing directly across the beam, begin approaching the mark from 10-15 boat lengths away. Immediately angle the boat slightly upwind. Finding the proper angle will depend on the wind velocity and how your boat is affected by its windage. Try using equal, forward throttle on both engines and steering with the rudders.

Stop the boat with reverse thrust on both engines. To maintain position, use a little forward thrust on the leeward engine, and/or reverse thrust with the starboard engine. Since reverse thrust is not usually as efficient as forward thrust, the reversed windward engine may need more throttle. Once stopped the bow will not remain where you pointed it — the wind will quickly blow it downwind. Turning toward the wind will help keep the bow pointing more to windward. Even with two engines and your newly acquired maneuvering skills, it is nearly impossible to maintain a position stopped beside a marker with the wind on your beam. Don't demand more of yourself than is physically possible but repeat the exercise enough times to learn its lessons.

LEEWAY EXERCISE

Comparing performance with boards up and boards down will be impossible for boats with-out boards. If you don't have them, try the exercise once just to get the feel of your boat's leeway.

Let's try motoring across the wind and/or current slowly. First, do it with the boards up. Pick an object (let's assume you were heading for a green day mark) on the other side of the bay, harbor, etc. Point the bows toward it and start motoring. Lock the helm off in the neutral position and set the throttles to identical RPMs.

Before long if the cur-rent/wind is strong enough, you will notice the heading you took will not get you to your destina-tion. You are no longer pointing at the green day mark. All the time you motor ahead you also drift sideways. To get to the destination you will have to point the bow higher into the wind, the way you did in the last exercise.

Try the same thing again with the boards down. This time, assuming the wind/current hasn't changed significantly, you will notice less drift. You would still

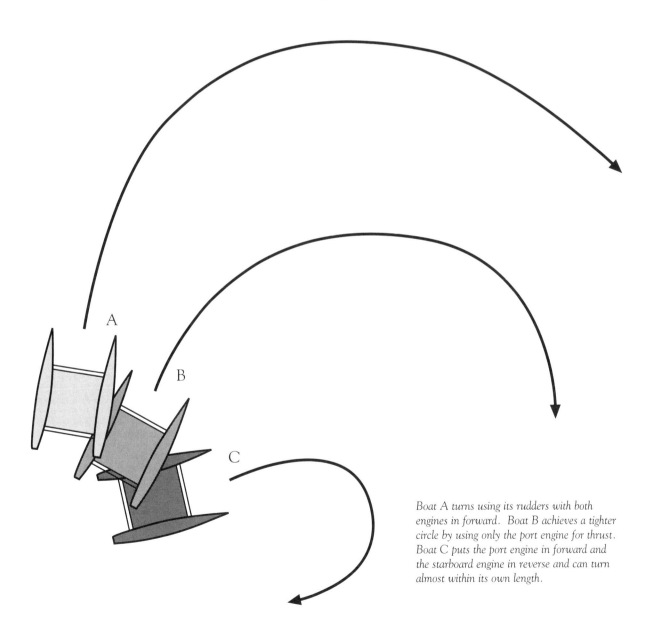

Boat A turns using its rudders with both engines in forward. Boat B achieves a tighter circle by using only the port engine for thrust. Boat C puts the port engine in forward and the starboard engine in reverse and can turn almost within its own length.

have to make that crab-like forward-sideways angle to reach the mark, but not as much as you did with the boards up. By the way, in both cases, higher speed will expose you to the crosswind for a shorter time and you won't drift as far downwind. Your crabbing angle won't be as severe.

TURNING RADIUS EXERCISE

Let's see just how sharply the boat will turn. First, try making as tight a circle to starboard as you can with the board(s) up with both engines in forward. Note the radius of the turn.

Next, put the board(s) down and try again (boats without boards skip this). You should see a much tighter turning circle.

Now try the same thing and keep your starboard engine in neutral. Notice the turning radius is much smaller. Now the ultimate — turn the helm to the right and put the starboard engine in reverse. The boat should turn a complete 360-degree circle within its own length.

Try the same thing in the opposite direction. Depending on the direction of prop rotation, you may see differences in turning to port or starboard. It's good to know if the boat turns tighter to one side than it does to the other. In close quarters turning in the tighter direction becomes a critical choice.

Now, try the same exercises in reverse.

BACKING IN A STRAIGHT LINE

The next task is to back up about ten boat lengths in a straight line. The engines by themselves will do the job. But experiment with the helm as well. You will notice that with both engines set at the same throttle position, and the helm straight,

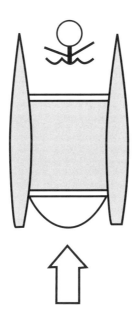

With a high bridgedeck and without swells, an overboard victim might be able to be safely recovered from between the hulls. A line between the sterns will allow people onboard to get the boat attached to the victim.

you should have no trouble going straight back. If you want to turn slightly, you can use the helm. Or, if you prefer, leave the helm centered and use only throttle control. If the stern starts to kick to the left, turn the wheel to the right. That will make the back edge of the rudders point to the right. With the water coming across the rudders in that manner, the stern should start coming back to the right. Take extra care not to leave the wheel unattended. Water pushing against the rudders can slam them against their stops and cause serious damage.

You may also want to experiment using engine power to counteract rudder angle. Can you turn the rudder slightly and counteract its effect with throttle adjustments? By now you should be able to apply your basic maneuvering concepts to such a task.

PERSON OVERBOARD

Some catamarans which do not have bridge decks, beams, nacelles, dolphin strikers, anchors, etc. within 3 feet of the water in the prevailing conditions may be able to safely recover an overboard victim by bringing him or her between the hulls. In general, this technique will only work safely with cats in the 40 foot or larger range. Consider this approach only in conditions when there is absolutely no possibility the wind and waves could bring the bridge deck superstructure down on the victim's head.

When the possibility of injury from above has been eliminated entirely, maneuvering the victim between the hulls has some advantages over bringing the victim alongside. Limited visibility on most cruising cats makes it impossible for the helmsperson to see the victim with the boat beside him or her. The spotter can help, but the possibility of hitting or overshooting the victim is increased by these boats' designs.

Higher freeboard and deck edges, which are often rounded, hinder the efforts of deck crew assisting a person in the water. Halyards and winches, the most immediate and efficient means of lifting a person out of the water on a monohull, are located a considerable distance from the gunwale on a big cat. It's just plain hard to work with a swimmer from the deck of most cruising catamarans.

The best place to get close enough to render assistance is the swim step/ladder.

Unfortunately, unless the victim has been secured to the hull with a line or some sort of rescue device, your odds of guiding him or her to the swim step aren't too impressive. Unless you have been able to get a line or rescue device to the victim, a last minute grab will most likely fail. Using a boat hook increases the potential of injuring a victim to such a degree that it should be used only in the most drastic situations.

Conversely, once the person is between the hulls with the boat moving slowly ahead, engines off and propeller shafts locked, he or she will surely come out between the hulls at the stern. A crew member on each swim step can hold a line between them and get it to the victim. If a crew member has to get in the water to assist a victim, a line can be tied between the two stern sections. The crew member can don a PFD, hook his or her tether to the line and easily gain control of the victim.

Landing Parallel to a Dock

Always assess the wind and/or current direction to determine which is strongest. Then make your approach with your bow into whichever is stronger. Again, always approach docks slowly. Remember the balance in your reverse thrust bank account is never as high as you would like.

Before approaching make sure you have a game plan for docking and all the crew are ready, some with coiled lines and others holding movable fenders. Have them tie other fenders in place.

With trailerables your docking strategy was little more than pulling alongside the dock. You watched for wind shifts and tried to pick the most favorable wind direction.

Twin engines add a whole new set of choices to the job of docking. It is possible to approach the dock from downwind and make an arcing turn which brings the hull alongside. Smaller boats with less displacement usually bounce off the dock using the fender as a cushion. Larger, heavier boats tend to crash into docks even when they are moving slowly.

A better tactic for pulling alongside a dock is to bring the bow in close to the dock, get a line on the dock and "walk" the stern in. This can be accomplished in a number of ways.

Again, wind and current forces must be considered. If you are being blown onto the dock you may want to bring the boat to a stop a foot away from the dock and let the wind get you the rest of the way.

This method will also work in calm winds or when the wind is blowing from the bow or stern.

Accidents resulting in injury and property damage occur at docks and in harbor areas more often than in open water. It stands to reason. That's where most of the boats are found.

Gaining confidence motoring to and from docks and around the marina will help you avoid most problems. After that, the open water's a breeze.

PERSON OVERBOARD DRILL UNDER POWER

You know the drill by now. Follow the same procedures you used in Chapter 2. A few differences that apply to cruising cats should be noted.

• Shift to neutral immediately when the "man overboard" cry is sounded. Propellers tend to be much closer to the outside of the hulls on a cruising cat. A person beside the boat with arms and/or legs under the boat will be much closer to the propeller than he would be next to a monohull.

• Go back into gear and follow return and recovery procedures (from Chapter 2) as soon as you determine the victim is clear of the propellers.

• The cruising cat's additional windage could affect your ability to return immediately.

• Use all the maneuvering techniques you have learned thus far to execute your return. A quick turn using opposing propeller forces may get you back quicker than turning with your rudders.

• Your spotter will need to give more frequent and specific information to make up for visibility restrictions on most cruising cats.

• Move gear shifts to neutral as the victim passes the bows.

• Turn engines off when the victim is anywhere aft of the mast.

• Shift to reverse when the engines are fully shut down. This will help keep the prop shafts from moving. You should approach slowly but with enough momentum to get to the victim.

STOPPING BESIDE A LEEWARD DOCK

1 Approach slowly at an angle less than 45°.

2 Bring the boat to a stop with the bow about a foot from the dock.

3 As the bow starts drifting toward the dock, shift the inboard (closer to the dock) engine into reverse in short bursts.

4 Alternate between neutral and reverse until the boat comes parallel to the dock. If it starts moving backwards use forward on the outboard engine while the inboard engine is in reverse.

5 Position crew to place fenders between the hull and the dock and others to step off the boat with dock lines.

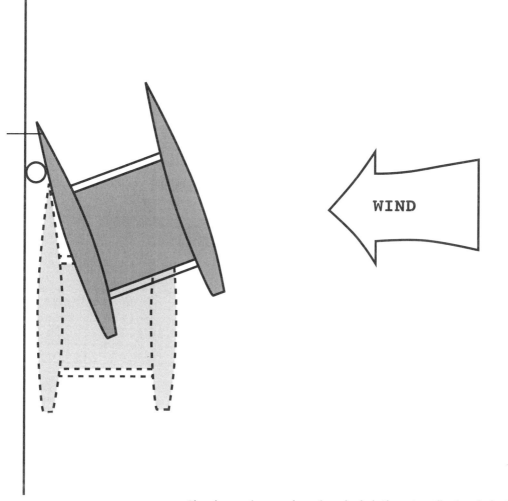

WIND

Short bursts of reverse thrust from the dockside engine will soften the landing as the wind blows this boat onto the dock.

STOPPING BESIDE A WINDWARD DOCK

If you need to land at a dock with the wind blowing the boat away from the dock, a running line may help you get the job done.

1 Approach slowly at an angle less than 45°.

2 Position a crew person at the bow with a line attached to a cleat near the beam.

3 Ease the bow close enough to the dock for the crew member to get a loop around a cleat or piling. Have the crew member hold the line fast.

4 Shift the inboard engine into reverse.

5 Secure fenders along the hull and position a crew person at the stern with a stern line.

6 Shift to neutral as the stern approaches the dock. It may take occasional spurts of reverse thrust from both engines to keep the line taut and the boat against the dock.

7 Bow–and–stern line handlers should step onto the dock and secure their dock lines.

Backing down on this running dock line will gradually bring the boat in beside the dock.

CHAPTER 7

UNDER SAIL

SAILING KNOWLEDGE

"The tree trunks used for small fishing canoes were so narrow that the tendency to capsize had to be counteracted by the addition of an outrigger to the hull. This consisted of a long spar of light wood, which rested on the surface of the water a little distance from the hull."

Vikings of the Pacific
–Peter H. Buck

SHALLOW DRAFT SAILING

Quite a bit has been said about draft, boards (centerboards and daggerboards) and keels. Trailerables seem to be able to float in anything deeper than a good-sized puddle and with their boards down, they can sail to weather like a fin-keel monohull.

Even many of the bigger, more sophisticated cruising cats offer this "best of both worlds" combination. They can sail comfortably in a couple feet of water and, with a little more depth, their boards go down and they can point and turn better than most people would expect.

Many manufacturers, in response to customer demand, have opted to eliminate movable boards in favor of short keels. If you decide to charter a large catamaran in Florida, the Bahamas, or the Caribbean, expect a shoal-draft keel. Charter companies believe their customers don't want to hassle with boards of any kind. They also tend to operate on a theory that says fewer moving

The addition of a stubby keel doesn't add much to the draft of this big cat.

parts = less damage and repair. You will still be quite satisfied with the performance of these boats and you will certainly enjoy the room and comfort they offer.

CRUISE PLANNING AND THE SHOAL–DRAFT CATAMARAN

While there are many places multihull sailors get to sail

that their envious, monohull neighbors never see, the opposite is rarely true. Sure a large cruising cat can't get into a standard slip, but who cares? There are plenty of places to tie up nearby. Would the monohull sailor have as little concern about missing hundreds of square miles in places such as the back country west of the Florida

Keys or large tracts of pristine waters in the Bahamas? It's not likely.

Board boats will need to consider point of sail and leeway in shoal areas. Let's suppose we are anchored on the deeper, eastern side of the Florida Keys and we plan to go through a bridge and head west toward the Thousand Island area beyond the Everglades. Our route will provide plenty of water to sail with our boards up but not all areas will allow us to sail with our boards down.

Before turning in for the night we listen to the following day's weather which calls for winds from the west. Some quick chart work reveals a northwest rhumb line that will put us on a close hauled point of sail. Without boards to resist leeway we can expect to track considerably further north than our rhumb line, possibly into waters too shallow even for our cruising cat.

If these conditions were likely to prevail for the foreseeable future, we could always choose to proceed as efficiently as possible and tack as many times as necessary to get into deep water. Depending on the particular boat, upwind progress could be tedious or nearly impossible. Another choice would be to wait for a weather change and sail with a more favorable wind direction. We could always motor but we don't want to talk about that in a chapter on sailing.

There are times when the charted depth in a shallow area may be significantly lower than what is listed on the chart. For example, when moderate to strong winds blow across a shallow body of water for an extended period of time, the water can simply get blown out. Extraordinarily high atmospheric pressure above a similar body of water can have the same effect. These are anomalous conditions but they do occur. Most likely, these types of events happen along with clearly recognizable weather patterns. Local mariners will probably be able to provide information. Even though your boat may only draw one foot, it's a good idea to stick to areas where the depth is double your draft or more. Chart data is far from exact. It wouldn't take much of a rock or coral head to span the gap between the bottom and your hull, even if the charted depth is correct.

Sailors don't cruise to get themselves into a crowd. We do it

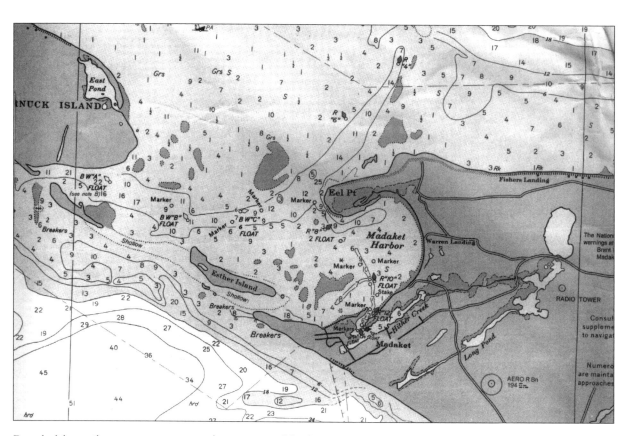

Deep draft boat sailors may never get to spend time in some of the choicest anchorages.

to get away from the crowd. There's no better feeling of having accomplished that escape than to sit at anchor in a harbor or bay, knowing your time will be spent alone or nearly alone. Multihull sailors can pick anchorages where their solitude is practically guaranteed. Why? Because multihulls are the only boats that can get to their location and, relatively speaking, there aren't that many of them around.

EFFECTS OF WINDAGE

Most cruising catamarans have pretty high freeboard which presents some large surfaces to the wind. At slow speeds in places such as a marina, you can feel gusts blowing you off course. Cruising cats with two engines should be able to handle most breezes pretty easily.

Windage at sea could have more serious effects. It could blow you off course and, over a distance of more than a few miles, it could land you somewhere quite different than where you wanted to go.

Chapter 6 examined course changes which become necessary with wind and/or current on the beam. Windage will also affect the boat's motion at every other point of sail. As you might expect, the larger the boat's surface area the more effect the wind will have on it.

Unlike current, wind will not have a 100% net effect on the boat's progress. In other words, whenever a boat is underway in current it will be affected by 100% of that current. A boat that can only motor at 3 knots will stand still motoring into a 3 knot current. Conversely, it will travel at a rate of 6 knots in the opposite direction.

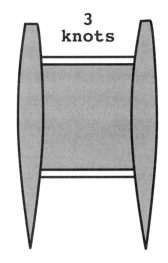

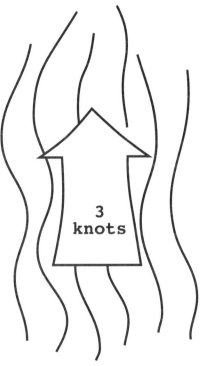

Making 3 knots of forward way into a 3 knot current will keep you right about where you started.

The same boat could probably make progress motoring into a 10 knot breeze although its speed would be somewhat impeded by the wind. The total effect of the wind would depend on the boat's windage. If it turned around it

would have its speed increased by roughly the same amount it was reduced.

Freeboard, spars and rigging may also contribute to the boat's propulsion under sail. As mentioned earlier, sailing on the hulls can move the boat without sails. The same forces continue working when the boat is sailing. In these cases windage actually adds to the boat's speed. However, there isn't ever a time (while you're sailing) when this effect is not occurring. Therefore, it is just considered part of the boat's performance.

Perhaps the most significant results of windage can be experienced while motoring. In general, wind will make you go faster downwind, slower upwind and unable to track precisely anywhere in between. Naturally, stronger winds will have more drastic results.

WEIGHT: CARRYING AND STOWING GEAR

Cruising cats, like all other sailboats, sacrifice performance for increased weight. We saw how much more stowage a typical cat had to offer in the last chapter. It's always a pleasure having cavernous spaces in which to stow gear. Just remember, any weight you bring onboard takes speed off your knotmeter. You can minimize that effect by distributing the weight evenly.

Tenderness to unbalanced weight decreases as a boat's size and displacement increases. Standing on the tip of a trailerable multihull's bow will cause it to sink under your weight. Bounce up and down and the boat will bounce.

Try the same thing on the larger cruising cat. A boat in the 40 foot range won't have much of a reaction to an average–sized person's weight.

Even though there's a vast amount of stowage capacity on larger catamarans, you still have to plan carefully. Keep the heavy stuff out of the bows. Don't load up one side more than the other. Your boat tour in Chapter 5 revealed stowage spaces throughout the hulls. Take advantage of the placement of such spaces when you stow your gear and provisions.

You also discovered holding, fuel and water tanks. While designers make allowances for this concentrated weight, partially filled tanks can change weight distribution. If you know you will be sailing with considerably less than maximum water or fuel (which isn't recommended), you can consider storing heavy gear in the area where the tanks are located. In general, the areas away from the bow and stern can more easily accommodate heavy gear.

Placing heavy loads forward in the boat, even in these larger, heavier displacement vessels, causes performance problems. If the wind picks up you will discover that the bows tend to dig deeper and deeper into the water. Heavier objects stowed further aft will counteract that effect.

On the other hand, if you are going for speed in light air, you will want more weight forward. Safety conscious cruising sailors will want any weight they shifted forward for speed easily moved aft when the wind picks up. Weight should also be balanced between the hulls.

The area around this tank can be used for stowage once the covering plate has been replaced.

> SEE APPENDIX A FOR SAILING
> KNOWLEDGE QUIZ

SAILING SKILLS

RIGGING AND SAILING

Smaller boats often "get away" with raising sails and sailing off the dock. It's easier to control the awkward moments between raising the sail and making way on a small boat. During that time the boom and mainsheet can swing wildly, the boat won't respond to the helm and movement isn't always predictable. The whole situation can get chaotic and somewhat dangerous to the crew and the boat itself.

Raising your sail at the dock is a great way to check reefing gear and other rigging, but sailing off the dock in a bigger cat can be risky.

It may be helpful to raise sails briefly on any unfamiliar boat while it is tied securely to the dock. You can find out if the last sailor put it away reefed or if any other running rigging will need attention. It's easier to sort that all out at the dock. As always, make sure the bow is pointed to windward.

Avoid sailing off the dock unless you have plenty of experienced help, plenty of sea room or you don't have a choice. It's simply a better practice to motor out into open water, come up into the wind and raise the sails.

These larger multihulls tend to follow the same trends in sail construction as do the smaller trailerables. Mylar and Kevlar are used much more often and fully battened mains have almost become universal.

Sail raising shouldn't present any unusual challenges other than the need to position the boom correctly for easier hauling. If the sail doesn't move easily in its track, adjust the topping lift up or down until the sail goes up smoothly.

You've discovered that the fractional rig creates smaller jib areas. Self-tacking jibs have become popular on larger cats because there's no need to grind yards and yards of jib sheet from one side to the other. Raise the jib and take a look. You may also find a fully battened jib on some boats.

There's nothing mysterious about a self-tacking jib. After raising it, secure the sheet and bear away. It will fill and draw nicely. Unlike the standard jib, the self-tacking jib has only one sheet. It runs through deck–mounted blocks which allow it to travel to either side of the boat's center line, depending on your tack. It may need trimming

A continuous jib sheet on this club-footed jib makes trimming quick and easy.

Once you're underway you can probably just point your cat at its destination and go.

JIBING SEQUENCE

1 While sailing on a broad reach the helmsman announces "ready to jibe."

2 Crew responds by manning the main and jib sheets and saying "ready."

3 Helmsman says "jibe ho" and begins turning downwind.

4 Mainsheet crew quickly trims the sail centering the boom.

5 Crew involved in the maneuver all watch the sails looking for the moment when the wind switches from one side to the other.

6 At the moment the wind fills the mainsail on the new windward side, the mainsail trimmer releases the sheet and estimates sail trim for a broad reach.

7 Jib trimmer:

  a. releases the old working sheet and trims the new one on traditionally rigged jibs

  b. watches and adjusts if necessary a self-tacking jib (in high winds or when the boat has been allowed to slow considerably, jib trimmers may follow #4, #5 and #6 to avoid an uncontrolled jib jibe).

8 Helmsman stops the boat from turning and gets it on course for a broad reach.

---

and you accomplish this the same way you do any other sail. Pull in or release the single sheet until the telltales fly correctly.

Once the sails have been raised and you bear away, begin sailing close hauled. If the boat has boards, they should be down. You will immediately notice the boat's acceleration and stability. Unlike the beach cats you have either sailed or seen, there's no hull flying even in a moderate wind.

Sail away close hauled and begin to get a feel for the boat's tenderness. What kind of helm adjustment does it take to stall the windward telltales? How much of a turn disrupts the leeward telltales? How does the wheel react under sail as opposed to powering? Explore the various sail trim possibilities using the mainsheet and boom vang. What effect do these adjustments have on boat speed?

All of this information will vary with different boats and prevailing conditions. Our discussion here could not possibly explore all the different possibilities. It is extremely important that you evaluate and learn each boat's peculiarities. Confidence comes from knowing exactly what to expect in any situation.

Bear away and follow the same procedure on each point of sail. Remember to raise your boards as you bear away beyond a beam reach.

The rudders may react differently on different points of sail. Lift on the rudders and pressure from leeway could affect their performance. You need to know the boat in each point of sail and in as many different conditions as might arise during your lessons.

JIBING

After sailing on a broad reach and checking your sail and helm performance, you will want to jibe. The trailerable didn't need the kind of mainsail control you expect on a monohull. Boat speed that nearly equaled wind velocity meant the main wasn't going to change sides with a lot of force. It would merely flop from one side to the other.

Your cruising cat will fall somewhere between the quick trailerable and sluggish monohull. You should get in the habit of using the kind of mainsail control you employed with a monohull.

Continue experimenting with points of sail on this new tack. Don't forget to lower your boards as you head up. The experience of sailing on this tack probably won't differ too much from sailing the same courses on the other tack, but you need to learn both.

TACKING

Don't expect any surprises tacking. The boat will have enough momentum to avoid stalling midway through the tack unless you begin tacking with very little way on. In such cases you should bear away to a close/beam reach to gather speed, then tack. The mainsheet should be tight when the tack is initiated, and eased when the bow goes through the wind. You may also find it necessary to de-power the jib and allow the center of effort to slide aft into the mainsail. With the wind concentrated further aft you add an important force to the tacking process.

In light winds your fully-battened sails may need help (open palm striking the sail) assuming their foil shape on the new side. If the wind is that light it probably won't make a heck of a lot of difference one way or the other.

Sail in a circle that requires you to tack, jibe and sail on each point of sail, until every crew member has had a chance to do his or her job 3 or 4 times. Rotate crew to any new positions in which they will need to function. It's a good idea to give everyone a chance to learn the helmsman position, even if he/she won't be asked to steer on a regular basis. You never know when you may need to ask someone to step in during an emergency.

MAINTAINING
A COMPASS COURSE

Most of the procedures for keeping a trailerable on a compass course will apply to the bigger boat. However, helm control may differ considerably.

For one thing, you were steering with a tiller on the smaller boat. It is almost universally true that tiller steering is more responsive than wheel steering. Unless you have a loose connection between the tiller and rudder, when you turn the tiller the boat turns. Wheel steering usually uses a chain like a bicycle chain and cables which run around pulleys. You may also encounter hydraulic steering which doesn't give you any mechanical connection between the wheel and rudders. Despite the best efforts of their manufacturers, wheel steering systems don't give you the same direct, responsive turning capabilities a tiller/rudder unit provides. You may have felt it already steering through the various points of sail.

Some developing sailors get confused making the transition between tiller and wheel. They conditioned themselves to steer away from the direction they wanted to turn with the tiller. With the wheel, although it is a very different mechanical device, you turn toward the direction you want to turn. Even if you already made the transition successfully, adding a compass to the mix may cause some minor set-backs.

Perform the same exercise you did in Chapter 3. This time do it on other points of sail and heading for different objects. Try making your corrections much bigger, say 40° or 50°. Then try making them much smaller. Can you make a 3° or 5° correction and maintain the new course effectively?

You will soon discover a small compass course change on a bigger boat with wheel steering presents a considerable challenge.

SAILING DRILLS

(Chapter 3 has diagrams for most of this work.) Place the marks further apart than you did for the same drill on a trailerable. Bigger boats often take a little more time to complete maneuvers. Avoid panic by giving yourself more room.

You will recall there were 4 ways to practice using these marks. First you can simply go around them leaving all the marks to port. Approach the right mark on port tack, trim and steer higher to close hauled, and tack. After the tack bear off and ease sheets to a reach. At the left hand mark, bear off, ease sheets and jibe.

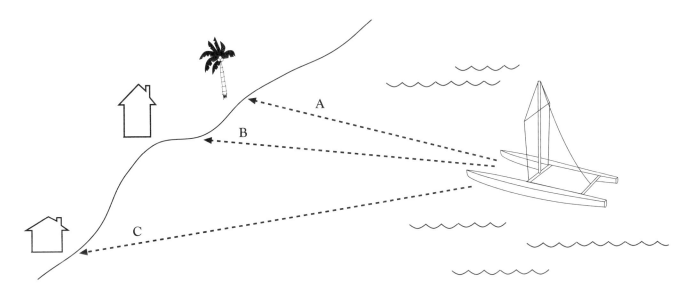

A course change between A and B can be more of a challenge than making a wider turn as you would between A and C.

After the jibe, beam reach back to the first mark and tack again. Keep doing it until the crew gets confident then reverse the process and sail the circle clockwise.

The exercise will differ from the same procedure on a trailerable in all the ways simply sailing the bigger boat differs from sailing the smaller boat. You will also find the cruising cat doesn't accelerate as quickly after it has lost its momentum tacking or jibing. You already have the marks further apart, so after you get the hang of this course, move them closer together.

FIGURE 8 PRACTICE

A figure 8 calls for the initial tack, leaving the right mark to port. After the tack, bear off to a reach and then a broad reach. Approach the left mark from downwind and make a starboard rounding. Here you begin heading up and trimming sheets until close hauled and tack again. Bear off to a reach, broad reach, and approach the right mark for a port rounding, head up and trim for a close hauled course. Repeat the process until it becomes second nature.

Finally, make plans to avoid bearing away to a broad reach after one of the tacks. Instead, beam reach away and prepare to bear away after you pass the second mark. This will set you up for a jibe.

After jibing, head up and sail to windward of the other mark. When you pass it, bear away and jibe again. Continue this figure 8 process and you will jibe each time you round a mark.

OBSERVING SAIL POWER

Try sailing along at full speed on a close reach. These boats really move. Now release both sails and let them luff. Observe how quickly the boat comes to a stop. Had this been a monohull the ballast would provide enough momentum to move the boat much further after the driving force was removed. Not so with multihulls — they simply don't have the extra weight. This is why some catamarans are somewhat more difficult to tack — they are so light they lose their momentum halfway through the turn.

To put way back on, trim the jib before the mainsail. What would happen if the mainsail was sheeted first? It would act like a wind vane and force the bows right into the wind — and we would go into irons. Always sheet the jib ahead of the main.

Now watch how fast the boat accelerates. Again, due to its lightness, the boat takes a lot less power to get that burst of speed.

In many cases, long distance sailing is simpler than cruising around the harbor and going to and from a dock. Naturally, open water sailing can present some big challenges but they are mostly weather related and most can be avoided. Repeating all the motoring and sailing drills in your harbor or marina or just outside the harbor will build skill and confidence. If you sharpen your skills close to home, you will be able to apply them anywhere in the world you sail.

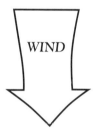

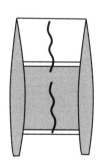

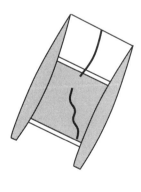

Jib sheet is released before the tack (left), and trimmed first after the tack (right).

CHAPTER 8

CRUISING

SAILING KNOWLEDGE

"The amazing fact is that somehow the Polynesians managed to navigate their small craft across hundreds of miles of empty ocean. Their only guides were natural ones: the sun, the clouds, the moon and stars, the waves and winds, and the flight of migratory birds."

Pacific Voyages
–John Gilbert

SAFETY

Safety harnesses and jack lines won't differ much between trailerables and cruising cats. However, you may want to consider alternative methods of running jack lines.

Depending on your tether length you may be able to travel the entire deck along a jack line that runs from a bow cleat to a stern cleat. If not, you may want to cross the jack lines at the mast or at a midship cleat. In so doing, each line starts on one side of the boat and ends on the other. You gain the advantage of close access to the mast which is the most likely area forward of the cockpit to require a visit. In addition, the forward bridge deck, including the forestay area, should become more accessible. One disadvantage of crossing jack lines is that you may have to unclip from one and clip onto the other outside the cockpit. A firm grip on the new jack line and a quick release "D" ring should minimize any momentary danger.

Please refer to the

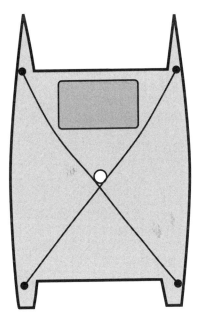

Jack lines crossed at the mast improve access to strategic portions of the deck.

International Marine Publishing book *Cruising Fundamentals* by Harry Munns for a more comprehensive treatment of personal safety and safety gear.

HEAVY WEATHER SAILING

Multihulls will reach high speeds in heavy winds even with shortened sails. While sailing to windward in a blow you will probably begin to encounter large seas. Depending on the distance between waves, you may have to alter your sailing technique. If the seas are very steep and close, try easing off the sails to take way off. Otherwise, you will find yourself banging hard into each of these short, steep waves.

If the seas are large and the wave crests are far enough apart, you can sail very smoothly while close hauled. Be sure never to sail so close to the wind you might go into irons. You could slow down or accidentally tack while the crew is not prepared. If you find the windward hull begins to raise due to freshening wind or a puff, spill air from the main as a short term defense. You could apply downhaul to flatten the sail or dump wind by easing the traveler or mainsheet.

When the winds are really heavy, you should not try to sail on a reach of any kind. The combination of heavy gusts and waves could cause a lot of problems. For example, if a huge gust were to hit and lift the windward hull and a wave hits at the same time, the boat could really get pitched high up on its side. Once it was up in that position, another gust could catch the boat from underneath and land that killer blow to put the boat all the way over.

In conditions where it is safe or necessary to sail on a broad reach, head the boat deeper down in gusts. This is just the opposite of what you do while going to weather. Remember, upwind when the hull or ama began to fly, you headed up. Here, heading up puts the wind and waves on your beam where you do not want to concentrate force.

Motoring in heavy seas creates its own set of challenges. If you find yourself motoring straight into steep waves, try altering course 10-30 degrees to decrease pounding. If necessary, "tack" under power to get to your destination.

Capsizing

The suspicion of instability discussed in Chapter 3 probably doesn't extend to cruising cats, at least to the same degree it exists with trailerables. Anyone who has stepped onto one of these larger cats soon realizes it feels like a monohull underneath your weight. It's solid.

Most multihulls will not capsize even under intense condi-tions. The conditions most likely to flip a large cat are high winds with waves at short intervals. Monohulls would experience their most dangerous conditions in similar circumstances. Generally speaking, large cats would not fare as well as monohulls under the same extreme storm intensity.

Most cruising cat manufacturers build their bridgedeck/beam/hull connections to withstand high stress. It wasn't always that way. Unfortunately, it took a few disasters to point out engineering weaknesses.

Even with structural improvements the basic principles of multihull design have inherent risks. The mere fact you have two buoyant hulls, each with considerable mass held 15 or more feet apart by 2 or 3 beams, creates potential for weakness. When

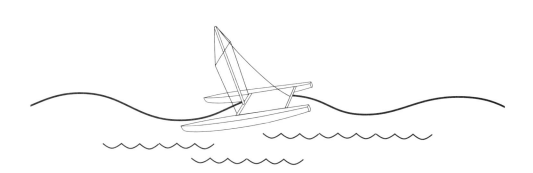

Waves that crest close together require speed adjustments that get the boat in step with the waves.

wind and waves slam into one hull with enough force to move it, the rest of the structure must react. Pushing a 1000 pound hull even a few feet, using essentially 2 or 3 points of attachment, creates stress at those points. That stress has been responsible for breaking up and destroying boats.

So what about capsizing? There is a point beyond which a catamaran cannot be tipped without capsizing. You may say the same is true about monohulls but even when they roll you still have an extremely heavy keel and gravity will not allow it to be held up in the air.

Your best defense against capsizing is still heaving-to with the bows about 45° to the waves (see Chapter 3). Traditional methods of heaving-to using a back winded jib and luffing main or reefed main alone may not work on large catamarans (you will try both methods in this chapter's exercises).

Pitchpoling occurs when a boat flips over moving forward because the bow dug into the water and the stern was lifted (it could happen the other way around in odd cases). It's a very real problem with multihulls because even under bare poles they sail downwind with great speed. When any boat sails faster than large waves on a reach or run, the bow could dip coming over a wave. Even dragging a drogue (dragging device used to slow a boat) or warp (long loop of line that slows the boat) may not slow a multihull enough to keep it from outrunning waves.

SEA ANCHORS

Sea anchor is something of an oxymoron because you obviously cannot anchor yourself to the sea. You can, however, attach

The area where the bridgedeck attaches to the hulls can experience extreme stress during heavy weather.

A sea anchor such as this parachute is essential to heavy weather sailing in a cruising catamaran.

the boat to something in the water with so much resistance the boat will stop moving forward sailing on its hulls and spars and make only about a half knot to leeward. These devices are called sea anchors or parachutes.

The sea anchor sits slightly below the surface. It doesn't go to the bottom like other anchors. You may hear stories about people dragging a tire (I can never figure out who sails with tires) or some other object that won't sink or be pulled willingly through the water. Most commercially available sea anchors are made of nylon or some other light, durable material. When deployed they are cone-shaped and act like a parachute except they fill with water instead of air. Some sort of rigid ring is often sewn into the open end. It keeps the sea anchor open and provides a sturdy attachment point for a bridle. Other sea anchors use only reinforced webbing at the open end.

You will need a relatively long line which will absorb some of the shock created by the wind and waves against the hulls. Anchor rode is probably good because of its length and durability. Guard against chafing as you

would with any anchor rode. Use shackles or thimbles which are plastic or metal guards that line the inside of eye splices. Wire shackle pins as you would with any anchor rode, taking great care not to leave any sharp edges exposed.

Use a bridle to keep the boat at a constant angle to the waves. The easiest and most versatile bridle can be made using a sturdy block and a line. A snatch block which can be placed on a line without having to slip it over the end might work best. However, because the snatch block has a mechanical clasp for attaching it to a line in use, it has another built-in possibility of mechanical failure.

The bridle line should be at least the length of the boat but 1 1/2 times the length would be better. Put the parachute in the water and drift away from it, paying out line. Secure the bitter end just as you would with any anchor rode.

Place the block on the anchor rode so that it can run freely. Tie the line, with chafe protection, to the block. Unless you want to man-handle it, run it through another block near the stern and to the primary winch on

what will be the windward side. You then adjust it, taking in or releasing line until you get to the desired (40-50°) angle.

Prevention is still the best cure so always pay close attention to the weather forecast and any change in conditions. Cruising cat sailors should develop a conservative philosophy of reefing for the anticipated puffs, not the steady wind.

The list of wind speeds and precautionary adjustments below resembles similar material in Chapter 4. It isn't absolute by any means but it may give you an idea of what to expect. It is well worth re-visiting this topic with larger catamarans in mind. Wind strengths are true.

15 KNOTS

With a full main and genoa, you should have nothing to worry about.

20 KNOTS

Watch for the leeward hull getting buried and the bow dipping while sailing upwind. A rooster tail may develop at the bow. In higher seas these effects may be more pronounced.

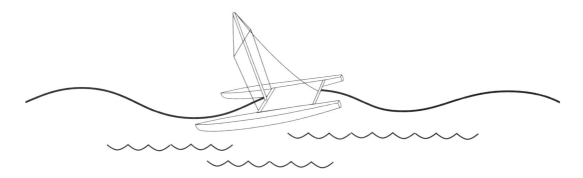

Waves that crest further apart present much less of a challenge to the cruising catamaran. Sailing up and down, rather than through waves, is always more comfortable and safer.

While safer due to greater stability, the cruising cat's galley still has to be navigated with care in heavy weather.

THE GALLEY

By now you get the message that one of the biggest things monohull sailors will have to get accustomed to on a cruising cat is "so much room." You have stowage room, sleeping room, head room (two kinds), cockpit room and room on deck. So why not galley room?

Why not indeed. Today's production catamarans have tons of room, lots of counter surface, spacious storage, huge refrigeration space, and more. The multihull cook gets to see the sights while he or she participates in everything that's going on in the main salon.

You really can't appreciate cooking in a flat, smooth galley until you've feared for your life

Take a reef. Keep your hand on the mainsheet ready to spill the breeze at a second's notice.

25 KNOTS

Start to consider a second reef. A lot will depend on the sea conditions and your particular boat. If you have been carrying a larger headsail change down to a 100% or smaller. Roll in a roller-furler to achieve the same result.

30 KNOTS

The leeward hull is depressed further. The boat may tend to surf downwind and the helmsman should pay close attention to how the bows move through approaching waves. If you sail into waves as opposed to over them, pitchpoling (flipping over bow first) is a possibility. Speed needs to be reduced to avoid this. Take a second reef if you haven't already.

An agile, healthy overboard victim can help him—or herself up the swim ladder in moderate conditions.

30+ KNOTS

Sea conditions associated with winds of this strength create a perfect environment for capsizing and pitchpoling. Set a storm jib or go bareheaded with a third reef if your sail has one. It may soon be time to heave-to.

beside a levitating pot of boiling pasta on a 35° heel crashing through 10 foot seas. Sure, the cat moves erratically going 12 knots in 20 knots of wind. But if it was possible to measure such things, a 40 foot catamaran would register less than half of what a similar monohull recorded on the agitate-ometer. This translates to safety for the cook and predictable meal preparation for the crew. No more salivating for 45 minutes only to find out the impending gourmet delight landed on the cabin sole.

Violent motion in the galley can produce airborne projectiles, severe burns from hot water or food and injury from getting slammed around the boat's interior despite the added stability. Add a few flying forks and knives to the mix and the cook may opt for (hockey) goalie pads and a face mask.

Foul weather gear pants and boots offer an attractive alternative without the impact resistance. Tying into the galley with a harness and tether can help reduce

fear of flying. Despite the dampened motion enjoyed by multihull sailors, cooks and helpers should take all possible precautions in and around the galley.

SEE APPENDIX A FOR SAILING KNOWLEDGE QUIZ

SAILING SKILLS

CREW OVERBOARD

Man overboard return and recovery was covered extensively in Chapter 4. A new boat design means new challenges. As always, take time to perform practice returns using a fender or cushion. Here's a great opportunity to put the experience you gained in your sailing drills to work.

One of the most important aspects of any overboard return technique is the crew's ability to stop the boat. You became familiar with the boat's ability to stop in the last chapter. That experience as well as your maneuvering abilities will come in handy here.

As was the case with overboard recovery under power, the stern swim ladder/step should offer the least difficult means of recovering a person from the water. However, it will be necessary to get the victim attached to the boat with a line or one of the popular recovery devices such as the Lifesling. It could take some time to get the victim back aboard and you will want some kind of attachment while you're working on it. You might even use a spare line with a huge bowline tied in a loop. A lot also depends on the person's ability to assist him— or herself as well as general fitness and swimming ability.

Follow the instructions in Chapter 4 and leave plenty of time to repeat, repeat, repeat.

REEFING

The most popular trailerables offer two mainsail reefing options, single-line reefing and roller reefing. Don't expect to see roller reefing on many cruising cats. Greater mast height and boom length mean more sail area and the sheer weight and bulk of it make rolling impractical.

One of the most significant trends in production sailboats over the past decade or so has been ease of operation. You might say it started with roller-furling jibs. Once sailors of the late 20th century discovered they didn't have to risk life and limb on the pitching deck of a sailboat every time they wanted to head for

As long as sailors go into irons before lowering the mainsail, it will fall between the lazy jacks where it should stay out of harms way.

home, they started looking around for other ways to simplify sailing. Today most manufacturers can claim they produce boats that one or two people can easily sail.

Most cruising cats will feature simple, easy to operate methods of raising and lowering the mainsail without leaving the cockpit. In most cases someone will have to go forward to attach the halyard but that can be done at the dock.

They use what's commonly called a lazy-jack system. It's nothing more than a sort of basket made of line or light sail material. It covers a triangular area at the bottom of the mast/boom triangle. When the sail comes down, the lazy jacks, keep it from falling off the boom onto the cabin top. It's that simple. And, unless it's blowing a gale, your sail will stay inside the cavity created by the lazy jacks until you are safely tied to the dock and can flake and tie the sail. In addition, once the sail has been secured in the reefed position, lazy jacks contain the excess sail cloth.

You can also reef the mainsail from the cockpit. Here's another good reason to raise the mainsail at the dock prior to casting off. Jiffy reefing, the name given to the system which is run from the cockpit, needs to be pre-rigged. If it isn't, you could find yourself unable to reef without some dangerous acrobatics.

With the sail up you'll notice a line running from the cockpit, probably from your primary cabin top winch, up through the reefing grommets. Pull it in and out a little to make sure it runs freely. If your sail has double or triple reefs the jiffy-reefing lines may be color coded.

Reefing the mainsail dockside eliminates surprises later.

LET'S GO THROUGH THE REEFING PROCESS OUT IN OPEN WATER.

1 Sail the boat as close to the wind as possible with the jib trimmed.

2 Ease the mainsheet until the sail luffs completely.

3 Make sure the topping lift is hooked up (not necessary with a rigid boom vang).

4 Assign a crewman to lower the main halyard until the reefing point at the tack reaches the hook. In some cases, the reefing line you discovered earlier will bring in the tack and clew reef grommets in one motion. Otherwise, someone will have to go forward to put the grommet on a hook.

5 Have another crewman tighten the clew (if the tack and clew are not controlled by one continuous line).

6 Once the foot is tight, have the halyard crew tighten the main halyard.

7 Adjust downhaul, sheet in and off you go.

Locating this windlass aft of the forward beam keeps its own weight and that of the chain off the bows where it can hurt performance.

REEFING DRILL

Without lazy jacks all the material we took off the mast will now droop all over the cabin or deck and create a lot of extra windage. So you must get rid of it. Traditionally, there are grommets and ties built into the sail along the reefed foot area. If you find grommets, roll the sail neatly and tie it up loosely. These grommets are not reinforced and can handle very little pressure. If you don't find built-in ties, use small pieces of light line or sail gaskets.

HEAVE-TO

The theory and advisability of heaving-to have been discussed at length. Now it's time to see what it's all about.

Even though it's improbable you can heave-to effectively with your sails, you need to know the boat's capabilities in this area so you need to experiment.

Start by simply sailing up to a close hauled course, tacking and leaving the jib trimmed on the old leeward side. After going through the wind, release the mainsail and turn the helm back over as if to tack back. If the boat agrees to heave-to, you can now take all the way off, hold the helm all the way over and stay pretty much in one place relative to the wind direction. Your only progress through the water should be to

With the bridle attached to the anchor rode, bow crew has only to release another few feet of rode to transfer the load onto the bridle.

leeward. If you throw something (biodegradable) in the water and it trails off behind your stern, you are not stopped.

Next try lowering the jib and reefing the main. Use a combination of sail trim and helm adjustment to get the boat to a close haul-close reach position relative to the wind. You will be balancing 3 forces. Windage on the hull and spars wants to push you downwind. Wind in the mainsail wants to turn you upwind. Rudders can help find a balance.

ANCHORING

Basic anchoring skills will serve you well on cruising catamarans. There are a few subtle differences, however. For example, the helmsperson's position way back in the cockpit may hamper visibility. Use the communication skills you learned for basic anchoring, including hand signals, to bridge this gap.

Windlasses help contribute to the cruising cat's overall ease of operation. Anchors on boats in the 40 foot range start to get heavy. Hauling a 20+ pound anchor and 30+ feet of chain by hand makes for some severe back strain. A windlass gets it down easier and up much easier. Most windlasses have a brake which holds the chain in place. It will be located in plain sight and releases by turning counterclockwise. A hammer, a special handle or some other tool may be needed to release the brake. Hitting the gear/chain mechanism may help free a windlass that has been locked for a while.

Release any securing devices and lower the anchor gently over the bow roller. Be ready to apply slight pressure to the brake to keep the chain from running out too fast.

If the windlass is mechanical you raise the anchor by turning a ratcheted handle. Electric windlasses are activated with a button. Some have a button for both raising and lowering. Experiment with it before shoving off.

Also remember that in shallow areas 4 or 5 feet of freeboard clearance can make a big difference in computing scope. Six feet of water becomes 10 feet of depth from the deck. Scope for the water depth only could leave you with about half of what you want and dangerously too little for the conditions.

ANCHOR BRIDLES

While anchor bridles were somewhat optional on trailerables, cruising cats almost always use them. Catamarans that do any serious cruising will have a pre-sized bridle stowed somewhere near the bows. If not, the same rules apply. Use a sturdy line, such as a dock line, about 150% of the boat's beam in length. A "D" ring or shackle with chafe protection should be attached to a loop such as a slip knot or bowline in the middle of the line.

Tie the bridle to bow cleats before you begin anchoring. Make sure it runs forward of everything on the bow and rest it on the bridge deck near the anchor rode. Follow your standard anchoring procedure. When the anchor has been set and the engines shifted to neutral, attach the bridle to your anchor rode. If the rode is chain at that point, the "D" ring or shackle will attach to one of the links. If this portion of

With the rode eased, the bridle now bears the boat's weight.

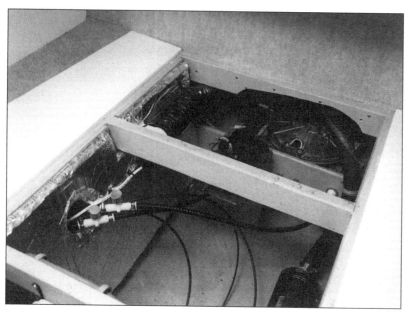

Cabin inspection plates may offer limited access to steering quadrants on modern cruising cats.

the rode is line, you need to tie a loop into it. A slip knot or bowline will work best. As always, tie the bitter end off to a cleat or pad eye.

Finally, ease the anchor rode out until the boat's weight rests on the bridle and not the anchor rode.

TWO ANCHOR SYSTEMS

Two anchors will give cruising cats all the benefits they give monohulls and trailerables. Setting two anchors properly reduces swing and increases holding power. Mediterranean or Bahamian style anchoring can be accomplished in much the same way you did it on a monohull or trailerable.

Once again, all that extra space on a multihull comes in handy. It gives you a big advantage setting your second anchor. If you set two anchors off the bow of a monohull as you did for a Bahamian mooring, it took some work to keep ground tackle and rodes separate. They both occupied roughly the same space up at the bow.

This is not a problem on a cruising cat. Your crew can prepare, lower and set each anchor on a separate hull. There's no tangle of lines and no necessity to completely secure and stow excess rode from the first anchor before setting up to lower the second. As soon as you set the first anchor you can change position to drop the second.

Once both anchors have been set, hook them up to your bridle, tidy up the deck and you're done.

Mediterranean style, with one anchor set in deeper water and the stern or bow attached to shore, is made much easier with twin screws. Determine from which direction the wind/current is coming and use your motoring skills to get yourself back to the shore.

In preparation, you will need to decide whether to go in bow or stern first. In shallow areas or somewhere where the tide will drop and make it shallow, head your bow for the beach. Bringing the bow in to a seawall or quay will also increase privacy. Most

places which allow this type of anchoring have lots of visitors who stroll around looking into boats for movie stars. It's a great way to meet new people but if you aren't in the mood, go in bow first. You will also want to use your bridle on whichever end attaches to the anchor.

Bow and stern anchoring can also help keep your cruising cat in one place. Unless you plan to use your dinghy for anchoring, you need one rode long enough to span the distance between both anchors. For example, if you anchor with 10 feet from the deck to the bottom, 7:1 scope would require roughly 70 feet of rode. After that hook is set you need to motor more than 70 feet away from your resting place to set the second anchor. Without 140 feet of anchor rode on anchor #1 you can't accomplish this task.

Hefty crew members can take the anchor out in the dinghy if necessary. The hard part comes when it's time to get the anchor up. Most dinghies don't provide a lot of buoyancy for doing heavy work over the side such as pulling up an anchor. If it gets fouled you may need to float the rode on a buoy and go get the catamaran.

You may also find it easier to set both anchors from the bow and walk the second anchor to the stern. This will be the skipper's decision and based, at least in part, on where the second anchor is stowed. You should also use a bridle for the stern anchor. Don't forget to figure the boat's length into your scope calculations.

EMERGENCY TILLER

Some sailing cynics believe every piece of equipment on a sailboat represents some sort of compromise. Everything that adds weight takes away speed and everything technical decreases the sailor's reliance on him– or herself. These same nay-sayers believe everything mechanical is something else that can break.

Unfortunately, anyone who has been towed in with a broken engine on a windless day or trimmed a sail by hand because a winch froze, would probably agree with the last theory. Steering systems rely on mechanical parts that can break. The time may come when you find yourself with a steering malfunction so you better know how to survive.

Your cat could lose control of one rudder and not the other. In such cases, you want to visually inspect the quadrants and determine if one or both is working. Just have someone turn the wheel back and forth while you watch. If one works and the other doesn't, you should center the broken rudder and find a way to immobilize it. The large, circular plate of the quadrant may have holes into which you can place a screwdriver or bar. Obviously, you don't want to force anything into an area where it could break something else.

You may also be able to clamp a locking device such as vice grips onto the quadrant and keep it from moving. The quadrant may turn freely as the boat turns in the water. If so, securing it will not be necessary unless you plan on motoring in reverse. The emergency tiller may offer one last chance to hold a loose rudder in place.

EMERGENCY TILLER EXERCISE

If the rudders are still connected to one another but not to the wheel, the emergency tiller will give back your maneuverability. Stop the boat in open water under power. Locate the emer-

gency tiller in a lazarette, locker or stowed in a compartment down below. Lay it out on the cockpit sole. It should be made up of one or two pieces.

Next find the deck plate or other access point. If you found your steering quadrants during your interior tour, check the areas in each hull which lie directly above them. It should be located near the stern of one or both hulls. There should only be one way the tiller fits onto the quadrant and allows you to steer.

Most likely the person steering with the emergency tiller won't be able to reach shift and throttle controls. Practicing with the emergency tiller will take some teamwork.

The shift/throttle person should get the boat moving ahead. Increase speed in 1 or 2 knot increments. Try making a few wide turns. Notice how easy or difficult it is to turn the boat at various speeds.

Next, stop the boat and let the wake overtake you. When it has settled down, shift both engines to reverse. Begin gaining speed as you did in forward. It should feel quite different. It may even be impossible to hold the tiller at higher speeds. Don't push the helmsperson or the boat beyond what it takes to make the point.

Now try motoring around a figure 8 course. Heading for a particular mark and getting the boat to move around it correctly should differ from the wide, arcing

The emergency tiller fits easily into the quadrant after removing a deck plate.

turns you performed earlier. This would be more like the type of steering you would do in and around a harbor.

DINGHIES

Even though your cruising multihull can get into shallow water, most of your time at anchor will be spent in deeper anchorages with monohulls. Unfortunately, you won't be able to walk to shore.

You will need a dinghy. There's good news and bad news on this topic as it relates to cruising cats. The good news is that most boats in this size range have plenty of room on the stern for davits which can lift the dinghy out of the water. The bad news is that if you have to tow the smaller boat it's probably a little more difficult with a multihull.

Davits raise the dinghy with a ratcheted winch (similar to the one on the trailer in Chapter 1) or a block and tackle system and a standard winch. In some cases it will all operate electrically or hydraulically. Always make sure the dinghy doesn't swing on the davits. Tie it tightly against any bracket that may be fitted in the area or into the davits themselves.

Use a bridle if you need to tow the dinghy. Towing from one hull can create drag on that side. To compensate you will have to turn your rudders slightly causing drag on the entire boat. The dinghy will also track in a straighter line with a bridle.

Dinghies tend to get active in any kind of sea and at the higher speeds cruising catamarans can reach. You can make a bridle by tying a snatch block onto the end of your dinghy towing line. Then tie a bridle line about 1 to 2 times the boat's beam measure-

ment onto stern cleats on each hull. Letting the block run along the bridle line ensures even pulling from both sides. Otherwise, your anchor bridle will do the trick.

CONCLUSION

In *The Great Gatsby*, F. Scott Fitzgerald wrote, "So we beat on, boats against the current, borne back ceaselessly into the past."

Sailing technology has yet to produce an innovation that isn't heavily grounded in the past. Take a look at boats from as far back as Columbus' time. While there have been many evolutionary steps since Caravels crossed the Atlantic, the basics haven't changed. It's unlikely the terminology and physical properties which dominate sailing will change substantially in the foreseeable future. In essence, multihulls are merely a hybrid strain of the basic sailboat, which is just a subgroup of pleasure boats in general. You can find as many similarities as there are differences.

By completing *Multihull Cruising Fundamentals*, you have added new and valuable knowledge and skill to your existing inventory. You may buy a boat, sail with friends, charter, cruise or race. Whatever your interest, the key to conquest in this or any other area of sailing can be summed up in one word, SAIL!

Now's the time to get up from your chair, tuck the book under your arm and get yourself onto a boat. You've learned all you need to know by reading words. Now it's time to read the wind, waves and sails. The American Sailing Association and International Marine Publishing wish you smooth sailing.

Whether you tow the dinghy or raise it with davits, it's a hassle until you need it.

APPENDIX A: CHAPTER QUESTIONS

CHAPTER 1

1 The trimaran's middle hull is referred to as the main hull.

　　　　True　　　False

2 The terms ama and aka describe the same part of a boat.

　　　　True　　　False

3 All multihulls bind their hulls together with structurally sound cross members.

　　　　True　　　False

4 The mast on a catamaran rests on

　　　A. the main beam.
　　　B. the aft beam.
　　　C. the forward beam.

5 Dolphin strikers help support the mast.

　　　　True　　　False

6 The headstay bridle would take the place of a headstay attachment on the forward beam of a catamaran.

　　　　True　　　False

7 Wing decks can be found on a catamaran.

　　　　True　　　False

8 Which of the following provides the most stable footing?

　　　A. an open wing deck
　　　B. a partial wing deck
　　　C. a full wing deck

9 Rotating masts allow for smoother air flow around the mainsail.

　　　　True　　　False

10 Trailerable production multihulls in the 20 to 30 foot range usually have wheel steering.

　　　　True　　　False

11 A multihull tends to heel less than a monohull because of

　　　A. buoyancy
　　　B. width of beam
　　　C. both A. and B.

12 When backing a trailer toward a ramp, turning the steering wheel in either direction will cause the trailer to turn in the opposite direction.

　　　　True　　　False

CHAPTER 2

1 Multihulls displace

　　　A. more water than comparably sized monohulls.
　　　B. less water than comparably sized monohulls.
　　　C. approximately the same amount of water as comparably sized monohulls.

2 Displacement has no effect on the amount of energy required to move a boat.

　　　　True　　　False

3 Movable weight concentrated toward the bows of a multihull helps the boat steer more efficiently by helping the bow cut into the water.

　　　　True　　　False

4 Each control line for the mainsail must have its own winch.

　　　　True　　　False

5 A heavily loaded line held by a sheet stopper or clutch should be wrapped around a winch prior to opening the stopper or clutch.

　　　　True　　　False

6 Which two elements determine a sail's aspect ratio?

　　　A. mast height
　　　B. mast and boom width
　　　C. boom length
　　　D. sail weight

7 The roach fills a small area near the tack of the mainsail.

　　　　True　　　False

8 The top of a square headed mainsail will get blown to leeward in a strong gust acting as a kind of reef.
      True   False

9 You want your "power button" as high as possible in stronger winds.
      True   False

10 A screacher is a light air sail.
      True   False

11 Headsails accelerate air flow across the leeward sides of sails behind them.
      True   False

12 Which of the following would describe the characteristics of an asymetrical spinnaker?
      A. an oversized, light–weight and loosely attached genoa
      B. a flat, "barn–door" type sail that pushes the boat downwind
      C. a light air sail used for beating and/or sailing as close to the wind as possible

13 Attaching the mainsheet close to the gooseneck helps maximize its pulling power.
      True   False

14 If you have 6:1 ratio mainsheet and attach a separate 4:1 ratio system creating a cascading mainsheet you will end up with
      A. 10:1 ratio
      B. 24:1 ratio
      C. 2.5:1 ratio

15 Boomless rigs do not provide enough sail trimming capability to make them practical on most trailerable multihulls.
      True   False

16 Ideally you want the jib lead pulling slightly harder on the foot of the sail than it does on the leach.
      True   False

17 Using a barberhauler
      A. opens the slot between mainsail and jib.
      B. reduces the load on the primary winch.
      C. closes the slot between the mainsail and jib.

18 Centerboards and daggerboards
      A. resist leeway.
      B. provide a pivot point for turning.
      C. both A and B.

CHAPTER 3

1 A daggerboard is raised or lowered straight up and down while a centerboard swings on an axis.
      True   False

2 Centerboards/daggerboards experience lateral pressure at nearly every point of sail except dead downwind.
      True   False

3 Windage is
> **A.** the average wind speed recorded on a passage.
> **B.** the angle at which a boat sails to windward.
> **C.** the amount of hull and rigging surface a boat presents to the wind.

4 A boat travels one mile across a bay and the trip takes 20 minutes. A second trip over the same distance takes 10 minutes. The same wind direction and strength were present both times. Assuming the boat experienced leeway, will it
> **A.** get pushed further off course during the 20 minute trip?
> **B.** get pushed further off course during the 10 minute trip?

5 Slightly over sheeting the mainsail and under sheeting the jib will cause less harm to performance than the opposite situation.
> True   False

6 If the headsail is sheeted properly the windward telltales would be dancing lightly and the leeward side would be flowing straight back.
> True   False

7 To correct your course when trimming by the telltales you must
> **A.** push the tiller in the direction of the troubled telltale.
> **B.** push the tiller away from the troubled telltale.
> **C.** experiment because all winds and sails are different.

8 A performance oriented multihull will get to a downwind destination quicker by "jibe tacking" from a broad reach to a broad reach than it would by sailing directly downwind.
> True   False

9 The mainsail will react the same way during a jibe on a multihull as it would on a monohull.
> True   False

Chapter 4

1 The U.S. Coast Guard does not approve any hybrid inflatable personal flotation devices.
> True   False

2 Jack lines are extremely effective in attaching an anchor rode to a sailboat.
> True   False

3 Potential for capsizing on a multihull has nothing to do with the power to weight ratio.
> True   False

4 A capsized multihull will tend to float using its trapped air and built–in flotation.
> True   False

5 The need to shorten sail will be as apparent on a multihull as it is on a comparable length monohull.
> True   False

6 When seas are steep and waves are close together you will want to observe the following:
> **A.** Accelerate to sail slightly faster than the waves.
> **B.** Bring down the sails and use the motor.
> **C.** Ease sheets to slow the boat down and sail in step with the waves.

7 If the seas are large and the wave crests are far apart you can sail very smoothly close hauled.
True   False

8 A trailerable multihull could get knocked over backwards by wind and waves.
True   False

9 Easing the traveler is not a good short term solution to being overpowered.
True   False

10 Sailing with the leeward hull or ama of an almost completely submerged trailerable multihull for more than 15 minutes would alert a prudent sailor that it may soon be time to reef.
True   False

11 You want to flatten the sail as winds increase.
True   False

12 Bending the mast flattens the mainsail.
True   False

13 In strong winds reaching is the least desirable point of sail on a trailerable multihull.
True   False

14 Rafting boats can be any combination of monohulls and multihulls.
True   False

CHAPTER 5

1 Cruising catamarans in the 30 to 50 foot range usually have forward beams.
True   False

2 Pressure from the mast to the main beam decreases when the main sheet is tightened.
True   False

3 A seagull striker takes upward pressure off the forestay/forward beam attachment point and disperses it along the forward beam.
True   False

4 Webbing or trampoline material is rarely used on large catamarans except, perhaps, between the bows.
True   False

5 Most catamaran designs have the main salon located inside one hull or the other.
True   False

6 Galley down refers to a method of covering all galley components to stow them for getting underway.
True   False

7 Rank the following 3 boat types from lowest to highest power to weight ratio.
    A. Cruising catamaran
    B. Monohull
    C. Trailerable multihull

8 An outboard engine will use more fuel per mile than an inboard diesel of about the same size.
True   False

9 Cavitation is
    A. a condition where sea life grows in any underwater cavity.
    B. a rolling effect created by steep waves while under sail.
    C. a condition where a propeller pushes air instead of water.

10 In general, which of the following has the highest probability of creating the conditions which could lead to an explosion?
    A. a bridgedeck mounted outboard engine
    B. an inboard diesel
    C. an inboard gas engine

11 Multihulls in the 30 to 50 foot range usually use two engines.
        True   False

CHAPTER 6

1 The nacelle is a molded fiberglass structure which protrudes below the bridgedeck.
        True   False

2 A nacelle would never have a hatch cut into it.
        True   False

3 Fractional sloop rigs are as popular with cruising cat manufacturers as they are with companies which produce trailerable multihulls.
        True   False

4 Sometimes, in place of centerboards or daggerboards, a cruising cat will use
      A. a high aspect ratio, weighted fin keel.
      B. a full keel.
      C. a shoal draft, partial keel.

5 Directly after tacking a cruising cat you always trim the mainsail, then trim the jib.
        True   False

6 A cruising catamaran under sail will turn more easily than a comparably sized monohull.
        True   False

7 Centerboards or daggerboards should be retracted to reduce drag and improve efficiency during a tack.
        True   False

8 Shorter dock lines help keep the cruising cat's more expansive superstructure tied more safely to a dock.
        True   False

CHAPTER 7

1 When moderate to strong winds blow across a shallow body of water for an extended period of time the water can simply get blown out.
        True   False

2 Unlike current, wind will not have a 100% net effect on the boat's progress.
        True   False

3 Which of the following parts of the boat will contribute to a cruising cats propulsion under sail?
      A. freeboard
      B. spars
      C. rigging
      D. all of the above

4 Tenderness to unbalanced weight decreases as the boat's size and displacement increases.
        True   False

5 A cruising cat in the 40 foot range will not have a very dramatic reaction to an average sized person jumping up and down on the bow.
True   False

6 Partially filled holding, water and fuel tanks can change weight distribution and performance.
True   False

7 Safety conscious, cruising sailors will want movable weight they shifted forward easily moved aft when the wind picks up.
True   False

Chapter 8

I In some cases crossing jack lines at the mast will improve access to strategic deck areas for tethered crew.
True   False

2 Basic safety rules for sailing in heavy weather differ significantly between trailerable multihulls and cruising cats.
True   False

3 In high wind conditions where it is safe and necessary to sail at a broad reach, it is advisable to head the boat deeper down in gusts.
True   False

4 Generally speaking, large cats will not fare as well as comparably sized monohulls in intense storm conditions.
True   False

5 Your best defense against capsizing is still heaving–to with your bows about 45° to the waves.
True   False

6 Pitchpoling occurs when a boat flips over moving forward as the bows dig into the water and the stern is lifted.
True   False

7 A sea anchor works on the same principle as a traditional anchor using scope and having the rode angle downward.
True   False

8 Thimbles are plastic or metal guards that line the inside of eye splices.
True   False

9 A snatch block has a mechanical clasp for attaching it to a line in use.
True   False

10 Bridles are rarely necessary when using a sea anchor.
True   False

11 There really isn't much difference between galley environment on cruising catamarans and monohulls.
True   False

APPENDIX B: ANSWERS TO CHAPTER QUESTIONS

CHAPTER 1

1. T
2. F
3. T
4. A
5. T
6. T
7. F
8. C
9. T
10. F
11. C
12. T

CHAPTER 2

1. B
2. F
3. F
4. F
5. T
6. A&C
7. F
8. T
9. F
10. T
11. T
12. A
13. F
14. B
15. F
16. T
17. A
18. C

CHAPTER 3

1. T
2. T
3. C
4. A
5. T
6. T
7. A
8. T
9. F

CHAPTER 4

1. F
2. F
3. F
4. T
5. F
6. C
7. T
8. T
9. F
10. F
11. T
12. T
13. T
14. T

CHAPTER 5

1. T
2. F
3. T
4. T
5. F
6. F
7. B, A, C
8. T
9. C
10. C
11. T

CHAPTER 6

1. T
2. F
3. T
4. C
5. F
6. F
7. F
8. F

CHAPTER 7

1. T
2. T
3. D
4. T
5. T
6. T
7. T

CHAPTER 8

1. T
2. T
3. T
4. T
5. T
6. T
7. T
8. T
9. T
10. F
11. F

APPENDIX C: GLOSSARY

Aft beam — Cross beam between the stern sections of two hulls on a catamaran.

Aka — Beams that connect the hulls on a trimaran.

Ama — The two outer hulls on a trimaran.

Apparent Wind — The wind strength and direction measured from the deck of a boat. The boat's speed and direction alter the affect of the true wind.

Backwinding — Directing wind and force onto the back or low pressure side of a sail.

Bearings — The direction from one object to another measured in either true or magnetic degrees.

Bolt Rope — A line sewn into the luff or foot of a sail which allows the sail to be secured in a groove along a spar.

Bridgedeck — The main structure spanning between the hulls on a catamaran.

Bridle–line — A line used for towing or anchoring on a catamaran. It has each end tied to one hull and a loop in the middle.

Bridlewire — A bridle which attaches the forestay to each hull on a catamaran.

Bulkhead — A vertical partition in a hull that strengthens and/or separates.

Cabin — Living space within the structure of a boat.

Catamaran — A boat with two hulls of approximately the same size.

Cross Beam — Any of the three beams that connects the two hulls of a catamaran.

Cunningham — Block and tackle system used to exert tension on the luff of a sail.

Dolphin Striker — Cables suspended below the deck that support the structure of a multihull.

Fairlead — A fitting used to guide a line in a particular direction.

Fairway — A major channel or portion of a major channel used for navigation.

Float — Generic name given to a multihull's ama or hull.

Forward Beam — Cross beam between the bow sections of two hulls on a catamaran.

Full Wing Deck — Solid structure spanning between the main hull and ama on a trimaran.

Headfoil — A metal extrusion fitted on a forestay and used to secure the luff of a sail by holding its bolt rope in place.

Jacklines — Lines running along the deck between the bow and stern used to attach a tether from a safety harness.

Lateral Resistance — The force that stops the hull from sliding sideways in the water.

Lazarette — Compartment in the stern of a boat used for storage.

Lee Helm — The tendency of a sailboat to turn away from the wind. The rudder must be held at an angle to keep the boat from rounding–up.

Lee Shore — Any land that lies to leeward of your position on a boat.

Leeway — A tendency for a sailboat to get pushed downwind while sailing on any point of sail other than running.

Lubber Line — A line on the compass aligned with the center line of the boat that indicates the boat's heading on the compass.

Main Beam — Cross beam between the middle sections of two hulls on a catamaran. The mast usually sits on it.

Main Hull — The middle hull on a trimaran.

Masthead — Top of the mast.

Mizzen — A sail located on a smaller, aft–mounted mast on a ketch or yawl.

Multihull — A boat with more than one hull.

Nacelle — Any hollow compartment created by the structure of the bridgedeck or a beam.

Navigation Rules — The complete set of published rules governing navigation.

Open Wing Deck — Structure spanning between the main hull and ama on a trimaran which is constructed primarily of netting or trampoline material.

Outhaul — A control line that exerts force along the foot of a sail pulling the clew away from the tack.

Pad Eye — A loop shaped fitting used to secure a line to some part of the boat.

Parachute Anchor — A parachute used in the water to slow a boat's speed.

Partial Wing Deck — Structure spanning between the main hull and ama on a trimaran which is constructed of both solid material and netting or trampoline material.

Pitchpole — Capsizing a boat bow over stern or stern over bow.

Pointing — Sailing as close to the wind as possible.

Preventer — A line, often the boom vang, used to hold the boom in place while reaching or running, preventing an uncontrolled boom swing during an accidental jibe.

Prop Walk — Sideward force created by a spinnning propeller.

Range — The distance a boat can travel using the fuel it can store.

Reef — Reducing sail area.

Rig — The mast and its attendant hardware.

Rigging — Cable and line supporting the mast.

Roach — The aft portion of a sail that extends beyond a line from the clew to the head.

Rode — Anchor chain, cable or line.

Roller Furling — A window shade–like device that rolls a sail up for storage.

Roller Reefing — Reducing sail area by rolling it around the boom.

Running Rigging — Adjustable sail controls.

Running Spring Line — Spring line which is adjusted from onboard the boat and used to position it on the way out of a slip or mooring.

Safety Nets — Trampoline material used to span the space between the bows on a multihull.

Seacock — A valve, operated by a movable handle, that restricts the flow of water in a line.

Seagull Striker — Rigid reinforcement structure on the forward beam of a catamaran.

Sheave — The grooved part of a block through which a line runs.

Stability — The tendency not to heel.

Stability Curves — Graphs showing the heeling tendencies of monohulls and multihulls.

Strainer — Filtering device used to remove solid debris from cooling water.

Strut — Metal fitting that supports and aligns the aft portion of a propeller shaft.

Stuffing Box — A fitting that seals and lubricates the propeller shaft in the area where it protrudes through the hull.

Telltales — Yarn or other lightweight material attached to parts of the boat or sails and used to determine the wind direction.

Tether — A line attached between a person's safety harness and a secure part of the boat.

Tidal Range — The difference in depth between high and low tides.

Track — The course a boat travels over the ground.

Trimaran — A boat with three hulls.

Turning Blocks — Horizontally mounted blocks used to re–direct a line on deck.

Underway — A vessel is underway when it is not affixed to land, moored or anchored.

Weather Helm — The tendency of a sailboat to turn into the wind. The rudder must be held at an angle to keep the boat from rounding–up.

Wing Deck — The structure spanning between the main hull and ama on a trimaran.

Chapman, C. F. *Piloting, Seamanship and Small Boat Handling,*
Hearst Marine Books,
New York

Clarke, D. H.
The Multihull Primer,
Granada Publishing Ltd.,
London

James, Rob
Multihulls Offshore,
Dodd, Mead & Co.
New York

Jobson, Gary
Sailing Fundamentals,
American Sailing
Association,
Los Angeles, CA

Munns, Harry
Cruising Fundamentals,
American Sailing
Association,
Los Angeles, CA

Pardey, Lin and Larry
Storm Tactics Handbook,
Pardey Books,
Vista, CA

White, Chris
The Cruising Multihull,
International Marine
Publishing, Camden ME

White, Rick & Mary Wells
*Catamaran Racing
for the 90's,*
RAM Press,
Key Largo, FL

Team Members Receive Special Preference

To our members the ASA means more than certification and educational excellence. It's smart business! When you join the ASA, you become a member of America's strongest and fastest growing team. Team members enjoy a number of important benefits.

HAVE CARD WILL TRAVEL
Rental and Charter Discounts

Nearly 200 locations across the country honor the ASA membership card and offer rental and charter discounts on hundred of different sailboats. In addition, some ASA schools extend discount prices to classes and other club activities. Whether you just want to unwind for an afternoon during a business trip or take the family on a cruisingvacation, your ASA membership card makes things happen. Discounts on car rentals and accommodations get you to your destination for less Go ahead. Explore!

SLEEP CHEAP!

Quest allows you to stay at over 1,000 hotels nationwide at a 50% discount. Just show your membership card and you will automatically receive a 50% discount on your stay at participating hotels. ASA team members are eligible for Quest membership at an incredibly low price. We guarantee you save more than the membership price your first night's stay.

ASA Gold Mastercard

The cardoffers one hour credit line increases, lost baggage protection, travel accident insurance, car rental collision damage insurance and much more. Competitive interest rates and no annual fee the first year make this one of the best cards available.

AMERICAN SAILING
The Journal of the American Sailing Association

Each issue of American Sailing brings you features on exciting traditional and contemporary sailing topics, navigation and seamanship articles, nautical book and video reviews, Sea Stories and more. In addition the ASA journal keeps you up-to-date on the latest in ASA activities and new ways to enjoy the sport.

Team members can shop for the gear and equipment they need at great savings. Most items bear the ASA *Sailing Team* insignia. Sailors worldwide will recognize one another by the distinctive logo. Equip yourself and your family with quality gear and equipment from some of the world's leading manufacturers.

In addition, receive discounts coupons for goods and services from these companies:

Sail Magazine	The Moorings Worldwide Charters
Bennett Marine Video	International Marine Publishing
K-Swiss nautical footwear	National and International Travel

The ASA constantly adds the highest quality member benefits available.

Your Membership Fee Helps Sailing Itself

Your membership in the ASA doesn't just benefit you; it benefits sailing nationwide. The ASA is a highly active representative to the National Boating Federation, the International Sailing Schools Association and the National Association of Boating Law Administrators. ASA strongly opposes restrictive boating legislation and works overtime to encourage fresh thinking to make the sport of sailing safer and more enjoyable.

Helping To Keep Our Waters Clean

As a concerned sailor you can be proud knowing that a portion of your ASA membership dues goes toward helping to clean up our oceans and to keep them clean. We select environmental groups that are dedicated to keeping our waterways free of trash that is so harmful to our marine life.

Join Today

Join thousands of other discriminating sailors who need to stay well equipped, well informed and wish to exercise some control over the sport and lifestyle they love. Don't wait - the team needs you!

Name_____

Street Address_____

City_____ State ____ Zip_____

Daytime Phone_____

❏ Check of M. O. ❏ Mastercard ❏ Visa ❏ Amex

Card #_____ Exp._____

Signature_____

❏ $39 one-year individual

❏ $55 two-year individual

❏ $20 additional family member, per year

❏ $75 one-year family (list additional members)

❏ $99 two-year family (list additional members)

❏ $300 individual lifetime membership

❏ $500 family lifetime membership (list additional members)

American Sailing Association
13922 Marquesas Way • Marina del Rey, CA 90292 • Phone (310) 822-7171 • Fax (310) 822-4741